The Complete Guide to
Insects and
Spiders

The Complete Guide to
Insects and Spiders

Jinny Johnson

Contents

A New Burlington Book
Conceived, edited, and designed by Marshall Editions
The Old Brewery
6 Blundell Street
London N7 9BH, UK
www.marshalleditions.com

Publisher Jenni Johns
Art Director Ivo Marloh
Managing Editor Paul Docherty
Design Schermuly Design Co.
Editorial Cathy Meeus
Main illustrator Gill Tomblin
Maps Mark Franklin
Production Nikki Ingram

ISBN 10: 1–84566–320–9
ISBN 13: 978–1–84566–320–9

Originated in Hong Kong by Modern Age.
Printed and bound in Singapore by
Star Standard Industries (Pte) Ltd.

10 9 8 7 6 5 4 3 2

This page Namib desert beetles, also known as fog-basking beetles, can "drink" moisture from fog in the Namibian desert.
Previous pages A leaf-footed bug, a type of true bug; An adult leopard lacewing butterfly rests on a leaf.

Introduction to insects

Did you know that a mosquito's wings beat 500 times a second, that a spittlebug can jump 100 times higher than its own length, or that cockroaches are among the most ancient of all insects, dating back long before the dinosaurs? Insects may be small, but they include some of the most extraordinary of all creatures. And in terms of numbers, they are the most successful animals on Earth. There are far more insects than any other type of creature.

Part of the fascination of insects lies in their adaptability. Because they are small, insects can make use of a vast range of microhabitats that would be unsuitable for other creatures. Insects are found all over the world and in every habitat from deserts to rainforests and from mountains to low-lying swamps. There are even a few insects in Antarctica. The only habitat that insects have not colonized is the sea.

How to use this book

The insects in these pages are grouped in chapters that correspond to the main insect groups. Closely related insect families and species appear on the same double-page spread. Individual entries are headed by the most generally accepted version of the common name of the insect family or species.

Text and illustrations clearly describe the individual insect species or families of insects covered by each entry.

Skimmer

Skimmers

Skimmers have a wide, flattened body that is shorter than their wingspan. These insects get their name from the female's habit of skimming over the surface of the water so that she can briefly dip her abdomen in to deposit her eggs. Found all over the world, skimmers usually live around warm and shallow, slow-moving waters.

The scientific name of the family is given in every case. Where applicable, the genus or species name is also supplied. The size of the insect (usually length; in some cases, wingspan) is given. The number of species in the family is followed by a summary of the regions in which the insect is found.

Family Libellulidae

Length $^{7}/_{8}$–$2^{5}/_{8}$ in (2–6.5 cm)

Number of species 960

Distribution Worldwide

A world map highlights the areas in which the insect is found, providing a visual summary of the distribution information.

Arachnids

Spiders are not insects. They belong to a group of invertebrate animals called arachnids, which also includes creatures such as scorpions and ticks. Arachnids also have extraordinary lifestyles—spiders build complex webs in which to trap prey, ticks cling onto and suck the blood of some animals, and a few kinds of scorpions have a sting that can be fatal to humans.

Essential to life on Earth

Many people think of insects and spiders as annoyances. It is true that many destroy crops, spread disease, and hurt us with their bites or stings, but they also are an essential part of life on Earth. They recycle dead plants and animals, return plant nutrients to the soil, and, most importantly of all, they pollinate plants. Some other creatures, such as birds and bats, are also pollinators, but without insects, many plants could not survive and whole ecosystems would break down. Insects and spiders might be small, but they are vital to life on our planet.

Above A honeybee covered with a thick dusting of pollen grains as it gathers nectar and pollen from a pumpkin flower. Without the help of pollinating bees many plant species could not survive.

What are insects?

Insects outnumber every other animal on Earth. There are at least one and a half million known animal species in the world, and about one million of those are insects. Some experts believe that as many as 30 times this number of insect species are yet to be discovered.

Most insects are tiny—under $^5/_8$ in (1.5 cm) long. They live in every type of habitat and they eat every imaginable type of food. Because they are small, insects can use a vast range of microhabitats that would be unsuitable for larger creatures. For example, hundreds of different species can live in a single tree.

We are familiar with insects and see them around us every day. Some people dislike insects because they eat crops and stored food, and some insects sting and bite us, and may even carry disease. Yet they do more good than harm. Their role in pollinating plants is vital to the entire living world. They are food for a huge variety of other creatures. We obtain products from some kinds of insects—silk, honey, and wax, for example. What is more, we can learn a lot from studying insects—particularly in relation to the fields of genetics and evolution.

Insect features

Most insects have the same basic structure, with three body parts—head, thorax, and abdomen. Typically they have six legs, two pairs of wings, and a pair of antennae but there are lots of variations. Not all insects have wings as adults, but all except the most primitive insects, such as bristletails and silverfish, have had wings at some point in their evolution.

Insects include creatures such as dragonflies, flies, bugs, beetles, and butterflies. Spiders and scorpions are not insects. They belong to a separate group called arachnids (see pp.132–53).

Below Two male stag beetles battle with one another for the chance to mate with a female. The beetle with the biggest jaws usually wins the contest.

The first insects

The first winged insects lived more than 350 million years ago. They were the first animals to fly, and insects are still the only invertebrates that can fly. Fossils show that some of these early insects were similar to the cockroaches and dragonflies of today. Some insects were fossilized after becoming trapped in muddy sediments, which later turned to rock. Others got stuck in resin oozing from tree trunks, which hardened to form amber.

Above This fungus gnat became trapped in sticky amber 40 million years ago. The amber hardened, leaving the fly preserved within it.

Insect anatomy and reproduction

Insects are incredibly varied but can be identified by certain features. An insect's body is divided into three parts—head, thorax, and abdomen. The head carries the eyes, mouthparts, and a pair of sensory antennae, which the insect uses to find out about its surroundings. The mouthparts are usually specialized according to the insect's diet and method of eating (see opposite).

Above Some weevils, like this one, have long snouts, which they use to bore into seedpods and other plant matter.

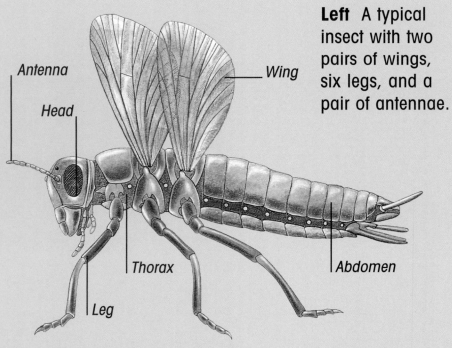

Antenna

Head

Wing

Thorax

Leg

Abdomen

Left A typical insect with two pairs of wings, six legs, and a pair of antennae.

Basic structure

One reason that insects are extremely successful as a group is that their basic body structure can be easily adapted to suit different environments and activities. Every insect has the same key structures on the head. In different species, these structures have been adapted for a variety of purposes. The same is true of the leg

structure, which can be specialized for jumping, swimming, digging, or running. In some insects, other body parts have been adapted to take on new functions. For example, the stings of bees, ants, and wasps developed from their egg-laying apparatus, and the silk spun by lacewing larvae comes from their excretory organs.

Exoskeleton and internal organs

An insect's body is enclosed in a supporting, protective structure called the exoskeleton to which the muscles are attached (see also Reproduction and growth, p.13). The abdomen contains the reproductive organs and most of the digestive system. Insects breathe air but they don't have lungs. Instead they have a system of breathing tubes that open to the outside through tiny holes, called spiracles, on each side of the thorax and abdomen.

Insect mouthparts

Insect mouthparts have become adapted for different purposes. The house fly's mouthparts are a kind of spongy pad, used for mopping up liquid food. Ground beetles are carnivores. They have large jaws (mandibles) adapted for piercing and cutting prey. In butterflies, part of the mouthparts called the maxillae form a tube for sucking up liquid food. Mosquitoes also suck up their food. Their mouthparts form a narrow, sharp-tipped tube. With this, the mosquito can cut into its victims' skin and feed on blood.

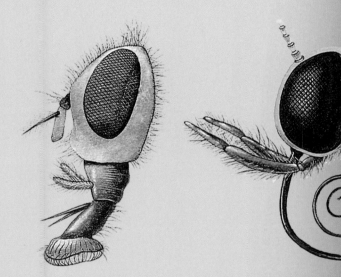

Spongy pad (fly)   Coiled tube (butterfly)

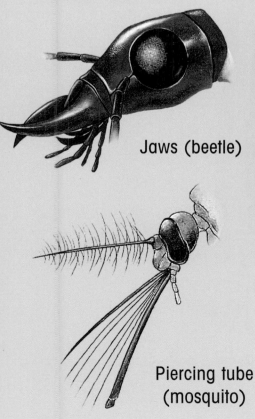

Jaws (beetle)

Piercing tube
(mosquito)

Below
Caterpillars have strong mouthparts for chewing plant food. This common swallowtail caterpillar is feeding on milk parsley.

Above and left
These examples of insect mouthparts illustrate a range of adaptations designed for different types of food.

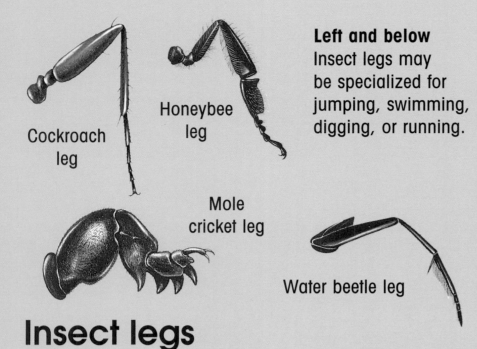

Cockroach leg

Honeybee leg

Left and below Insect legs may be specialized for jumping, swimming, digging, or running.

Mole cricket leg

Water beetle leg

Left Bumblebees visit flowers to collect nectar and pollen. They carry the pollen on specially adapted areas on the back legs.

Insect legs

The legs of insects are made up of the same basic parts, but vary according to the lifestyle of the species. For example, a cockroach's long legs are built for running and have backward-pointing spines for holding onto surfaces. The mole cricket's legs are short and spadelike—ideal for digging. The water beetle's legs are fringed with hairs, which help the insect push its way through the water. The honeybee's back legs are adapted for pollen gathering. Pollen sticks to the hairs on the legs and is collected into a special area on each back leg known as a pollen basket.

Insect senses

Insects have antennae and tiny sensory hairs that detect smells, tastes, vibrations, and sounds. Some antennae have many side branches to increase the surface area of sensory cells and hairs.

Most insects also have eyes, but sight is generally less important to insects than to animals such as birds and mammals. Many insects—for example, ants—also communicate with chemical signals. They can pass on chemical messages to each other by touching antennae. Some insects have very sensitive hearing organs, and crickets have "ears" on their front legs.

Ant antenna

Female mosquito antenna

Moth antenna

Cockchafer antenna

Above Antennae help an insect find out more about its surroundings. Some are branched to increase the sensory surface area.

Left The huge branched antennae of some male moths, such as this Chinese oak silkworm moth, help them pick up the scent of females.

Insect wings

In most insects, two pairs of wings are attached to the thorax. The wing membrane may be covered with tiny hairs or scales. In some insects—for example, worker ants and termites— wings do not develop. The lacewing has delicate wings with a large number of cross veins. In beetles the hard front wings form protective covers for the folded hind wings. A butterfly's wing is large and covered with minute scales.

Left An Asian lady beetle in flight, with its hard wing cases open and its hind wings spread.

Below This female spotted moth is laying her eggs on a papaya plant. These will hatch into caterpillars that will feed on the leaves of the plant and grow fast.

Reproduction and growth

All insects lay eggs. These hatch into young, which may be miniature versions of their parents or very different in form. In order to grow to adult size, a young insect must molt, that is shed its exoskeleton—the hard casing on the outside of its body. This happens a number of times during its life. A new skeleton forms beneath the old one, and when it is ready to molt, the insect splits the old skeleton and wriggles out. Some young insects, such as caterpillars, have soft exoskeletons. They too, molt several times before they grow a hard exoskeleton as an adult butterfly or moth.

Above As they grow bigger, crickets must molt and discard their outgrown exoskeletons. This great green bush-cricket is making its last molt and is now adult size.

Classification

Insects and arachnids are classes of invertebrates (creatures without a backbone) that belong to the Arthropoda phylum within the Animal Kingdom. These classes are divided into groupings known as orders. Bristletails and silverfish, for example, belong to the order Thysanura. Orders are divided into families, which consist of smaller groups called genera (singular, genus), which are in turn made up of individual species.

PRIMITIVE WINGLESS INSECTS

Bristletails and silverfish (Thysanura) 5,000 species

Key

Kingdom

Phylum

Class

Subclass

Order

Animal Kingdom

Arthropoda

Insects | Arachnids (see p.135)

WINGED INSECTS with incomplete metamorphosis

Mayflies (Ephemeroptera) 3,000 species

Dragonflies and damselflies (Odonata) 5,000 species

Stoneflies (Plecoptera) 2,000 species

Webspinners (Embioptera) at least 170 species

Zorapterans (Zoraptera) 33 species

Earwigs (Dermaptera) 2,000 species

Rock crawlers (Grylloblattodea) 25 species

Grasshoppers and crickets (Orthoptera) 20,000 species

Leaf and stick insects (Phasmida) 2,500 species

Cockroaches (Blattodea) 4,000 species

Termites (Isoptera) 2,600 species

Mantids (Mantodea) 1,800 species

Parasitic lice (Phthiraptera) 4,900 species

Barklice (Psocoptera) 3,000 species

Thrips (Thysanoptera) 5,000 species

True bugs (Hemiptera) at least 90,000

WINGED INSECTS with complete metamorphosis

Beetles (Coleoptera) 250,000 species

Alderflies (Megaloptera) 300 species

Snakeflies (Raphidioptera) 200 species

Lacewings (Neuroptera) 6,000 species

Caddisflies (Trichoptera) 11,000 species

Butterflies and moths (Lepidoptera) 160,000 species

Scorpionflies (Mecoptera) 550 species

Fleas (Siphonoptera) 2,575 species

True flies (Diptera) 124,000 species

Sawflies, wasps, ants, and bees (Hymenoptera) probably more than 250,000 species

Above An emperor dragonfly rests on a plant before flying off in pursuit of prey. Dragonflies can fly at speeds of up to 34 miles an hour (55 kph).

Dragonflies and relatives

These are among the most primitive of insects. One of the earliest of all known insect fossils is that of a member of this group, a bristletail, and is thought to date from about 390 million years ago.

Characteristics

Small insects with flattened bodies and no wings, bristletails spend their lives scurrying round in dark, damp corners and are not often seen. Females lay eggs that hatch into tiny versions of their parents. They may molt as many as eight times as they grow.

Mayflies and dragonflies do have wings, and they are also among the most ancient groups of insects. Giant dragonflies were flying in the skies 300 million years ago—before dinosaurs walked the earth. Most dragonflies are large, cclorful fast-flying insects that seize their prey in the air. Slower-flying damselflies are hunters, too.

Above This newly emerged adult dragonfly clings to a grass stem below its discarded skin.

Life cycle

FROM NYMPH TO DRAGONFLY

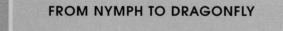

Eggs

1 Dragonflies lay their eggs in water.
2 The eggs hatch into young called nymphs or naiads, which live in water, feeding on tadpoles and fish.
3 When the nymph is fully grown, it crawls out of the water onto a plant.
4 Its skin splits and the head and thorax come out. Legs and wings follow, and finally the abdomen emerges.
5 The adult dragonfly waits by its old skin until its wings are strong enough to enable it to fly away.

Bristletails and mayflies

Bristletails, such as silverfish and firebrats, do not have wings and have never had wings at any time in their evolution. All other insects, even those, such as fleas, that are wingless now are descended from winged ancestors. Bristletails are named for the three threadlike tails at the end of the body. The tails are fringed with tiny hairs and may be very sensitive. These tiny creatures have unusually long lives for insects, and can survive two or three years or more. In contrast, mayflies are very short lived and their group name Ephemeroptera actually means "living for a day." They have one or two pairs of wings but are not strong fliers.

Family	Lepismatidae
Latin name	*Thermobia domestica*
Length	$3/8$–$5/8$ in (1–1.5 cm)
Distribution	Worldwide

Firebrat

Silverfish

Light-shy silverfish usually live in dark places, such as under tree bark or among rotting leaves. Many live inside houses, where they eat paper, glue, and spilled foods. They can run fast but cannot jump. The long tapering body is covered with tiny scales. Its flattened shape allows the silverfish to squeeze into tiny cracks and crevices.

Family	Lepismatidae
Latin name	*Lepisma saccharina*
Length	$3/8$–$5/8$ in (1–1.5 cm)
Distribution	Worldwide

Firebrat

Like the silverfish, the firebrat often lives in houses. It gets its name because it likes to live near the warmth of boilers, fires, or ovens. It scurries about looking for scraps of food and other debris to eat. Females lay their eggs in dark cracks. The eggs hatch into tiny versions of the parent and the young molt up to 10 times while they grow to adult size.

Silverfish

Small minnow mayflies

Adult mayflies do not feed and they live for only one day, sometimes only a few hours. This gives them just enough time to mate and lay their eggs. Mayfly larvae, however, live in water for a year or more before becoming winged adults. The larvae look a little like silverfish as they have two or three long tails at the end of the body. They molt many times before they reach adult size.

Small minnow mayfly larva

Small minnow mayfly adult

Family	Baetidae
Length	About $3/8$ in (1 cm)
Number of species	700
Distribution	Worldwide

Burrowing mayflies

This family includes some of the largest mayflies. The females lay their eggs on the surface of slow-moving rivers or lakes, and the eggs sink to the bottom where they hatch. The larvae dig little burrows into the mud and silt and live there, feeding on tiny plants and algae.

Family	Ephemeridae
Length	Up to $1 3/8$ in (3.5 cm)
Number of species	30
Distribution	Worldwide, except Australia

Burrowing mayfly

Spinner mayflies

Like other mayfly larvae, the spinner larva lives in water, feeding on plant matter, while it molts and grows for a year or more. When it reaches the last larval stage, it grows wings and leaves the water. It soon sheds this skin and emerges as an adult, ready to mate, lay eggs, and die. Thousands of mayflies usually leave the water together in huge swarms.

Spinner mayfly

Family	Leptophlebiidae
Length	$3/16$–$1/2$ in (0.5–1.3 cm)
Number of species	900
Distribution	Worldwide

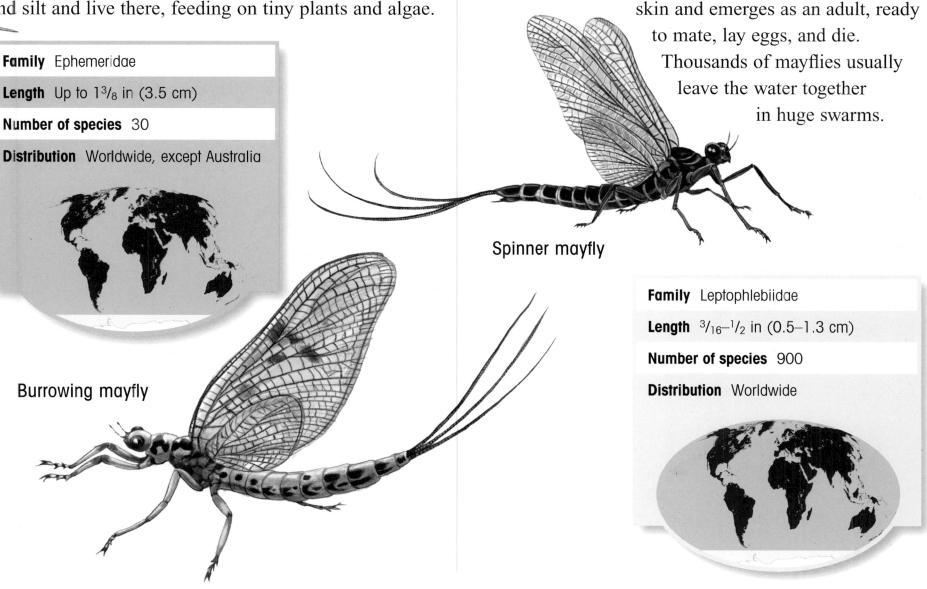

Damselflies

Close relatives of dragonflies, damselflies have long, slender bodies and two pairs of filmy wings. They fly more slowly than dragonflies and range in length from only 3/4 in (19 mm) to the giant damselfly of South America that measures up to 7 in (19 cm). At rest, most damselflies hold their wings closed above the body, not spread apart like dragonflies. Before mating, some male damselflies hover in front of the female to show off their bright colors. The female damselfly inserts her eggs inside a plant stem with her egg-laying tube.

Spread-winged damselfly

Narrow-winged damselflies

The males of these damselflies usually have brighter coloration than the females. Their larvae, like those of all damselflies, live in water and catch small insects to eat. The larvae capture their prey by shooting forward the long lower lip, which is tipped with sharp claws, to grab prey. When not in use, the lip—sometimes known as the mask—is folded up under the head.

Family	Coenagrionidae
Length	1–2 in (2.5–5 cm)
Number of species	1,060
Distribution	Worldwide

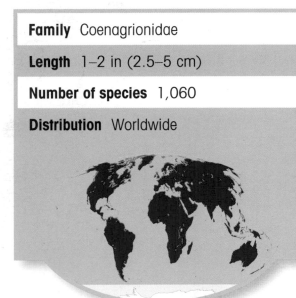

Narrow-winged damselfly

Spread-winged damselflies

These damselflies get their common name from their habit of holding their wings partly spread out when at rest. They are also known as emerald damselflies. They live around ponds and marshes, where they feed on insects such as aphids, which they pick from plants. The larvae eat small water-living insects.

Family	Lestidae
Length	1 1/4–2 in (3–5 cm)
Number of species	155
Distribution	Worldwide

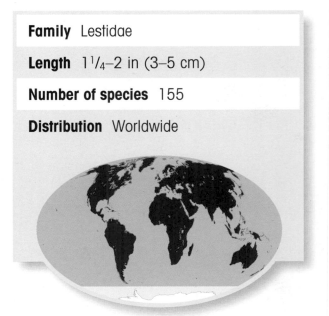

Broad-winged damselflies

These large, usually colourful, damselflies have wings that broaden out from the base rather than being on stalks. Most live near streams in woods and forests and feed on small insects such as aphids. Like all damselflies, the nymphs have tiny gills at the end of the abdomen (dragonfly nymphs have gills inside the body).

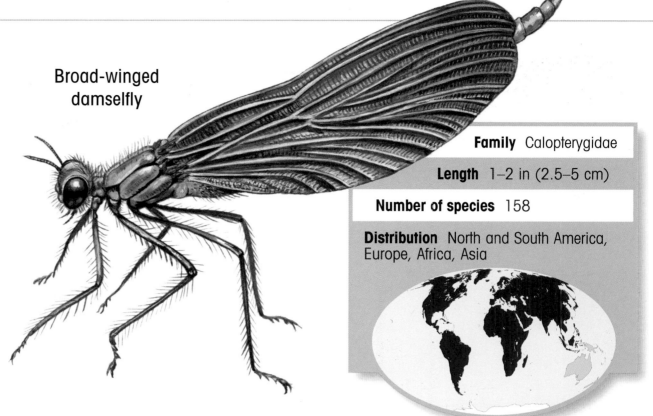

Broad-winged damselfly

Family	Calopterygidae
Length	1–2 in (2.5–5 cm)
Number of species	158
Distribution	North and South America, Europe, Africa, Asia

Banded demoiselle

This damselfly lives around ponds and slow-moving streams and rivers. The male has a bluish green body with a blue-black band on the wings. The female is green and does not have wing markings. Like other damselflies, the male banded demoiselle claims a territory which includes suitable egg-laying sites. He tries to attract females to his territory and fights off rival males.

Female banded demoiselle

Family	Calopterygidae
Latin name	*Calopteryx splendens*
Length	$^3/_{16}$ in (5 mm)
Distribution	Europe

White-legged damselfly

As its name suggests, the male of this species of damselfly has distinctive white back legs, which it shows off when it performs display flights to attract females. This damselfly lives around still or slow-moving water where there is plenty of vegetation. The female lays her eggs in plant stems or on the underside of floating leaves.

White-legged damselfly

Family	Platycnemididae
Latin name	*Platycnemis pennipes*
Length	$^5/_{32}$ in (4 mm)
Distribution	Europe

Insect flight

Insects were the first creatures to fly. The power of flight gives insects a huge advantage over land-based invertebrates, enabling them to escape more easily from predators and to travel long distances in search of food or a mate.

Ladybug in flight

Speedy dragonflies

Dragonflies are some of the speediest of all insects and can fly up to 34 mph (55 kph). The largest dragonflies have wings that span 5 in (12.5 cm) when fully spread. Dragonflies flap their four wings in unison for fast, level flight. By flapping the front and back wings independently, they can perform amazing aerobatics, changing direction rapidly, hovering, stopping in mid-flight, and even flying backwards. In normal flight a dragonfly may beat its wings 25 times a second but can make sudden bursts of more rapid wing-beats if chasing prey.

Above The front wings of beetles such as ladybugs have evolved into hard, protective wing cases. The back wings are kept folded under the wing cases and are only unfurled for flight.

Above An eight-spotted skimmer, a type of dragonfly, darts out from its perch at high speed to seize prey in midair. Although its wings beat slowly compared with those of flies and bees, a dragonfly is still an expert flier.

Other types of insect wings

In other insects, wings have adapted in different ways. For example, the front wings of beetles have evolved into hard wing cases that protect the more delicate hind wings. For flying, beetles use only their hind wings which are kept folded up beneath the wing cases until it is time for take off. The wings of butterflies and moths are covered with tiny scales. These scales are actually flattened hairs and they create the colorful patterns on their wings. In some, such as the sphinx moth, the wings beat so fast that the moths can hover in front of flowers to feed on nectar.

Front wing

Wing vein

Left Painted lady butterflies can fly hundreds of miles on their delicate wings. They migrate between Britain and North Africa, and between northern parts of the U.S.A. and Mexico.

Fly halteres

Haltere

Wing

Unlike other flying insects, flies have just one pair of wings. The hind wings have developed into a pair of clublike structures called halteres, one on each side of the body. These act as balancing organs. They vibrate, helping the fly to control its flight and change direction as it zooms through the air. The wings of some tiny flies vibrate 1,000 times a second.

Dragonflies

Colorful dragonflies are among the fastest flying, and most acrobatic of all insects. They are an eye-catching sight as they dart and swoop in search of prey such as flies, which they generally catch in midair. Their slender legs are not suited to walking, but are used for seizing prey or for clinging to stems or other supports. Dragonflies live all over the world. There are about 5,000 different species. All have delicately veined wings, strong jaws, and large eyes. They lay their eggs in or close to water. The young are called naiads or nymphs.

Biddy

Skimmer

Skimmers

Skimmers have a wide, flattened body that is shorter than their wingspan. These insects get their name from the female's habit of skimming over the surface of the water so that she can briefly dip her abdomen in to deposit her eggs. Found all over the world, skimmers usually live around warm and shallow, slow-moving waters.

Family	Libellulidae
Length	7/8–2⅝ in (2–6.5 cm)
Number of species	960
Distribution	Worldwide

Family	Cordulegastridae
Length	2½–3¹/₁₆ in (6–8 cm)
Number of species	50
Distribution	North America, Europe, Asia

Biddies

Biddies are large dragonflies, often seen near woodland streams where they hover about a foot above the water surface. They have big eyes that meet—or nearly meet—on the broad head. Both head and thorax are covered with fine hairs. Biddy naiads are large and hairy, too. They live underwater at the bottom of streams, where they feed on other insects and tadpoles.

Green darner

Green darners are among the largest and fastest-flying of dragonflies. When hunting they zoom back and forth with legs held ready to seize prey. The male is very territorial, patroling and defending a particular area. Females are allowed to enter this territory, but other males are chased away. Adult darners feed on midges, mosquitoes, and other flying insects, while naiads eat tadpoles, insects, and even small fish.

Family	Aeshnidae
Latin name	*Anax junius*
Length	$2^3/_4$–$3^1/_{16}$ in (7–8 cm)
Distribution	North America

Green darner

Clubtail dragonflies

These dragonflies have a different hunting technique from darners. The clubtail finds a suitable perch and watches out for prey. Once it sights something, it darts out to seize the victim, then returns to its perch. Clubtail dragonflies have widely separated eyes.

Family	Gomphidae
Length	Up to 3 in (7.5 cm)
Number of species	950
Distribution	Worldwide

Clubtail dragonfly

Emperor dragonfly

These large, broad-winged dragonflies are fast fliers and expert midair predators. Like all dragonflies, when at rest, they keep their wings outstretched, not folded away. The naiad, like those of other dragonflies, has a long lower lip, tipped with sharp claws, which can shoot forward to grab prey. When not in use, the lip—sometimes known as the mask—is folded up over the head.

Emperor dragonfly

Family	Aeshnidae
Latin name	*Anax imperator*
Length	Up to $3^1/_{16}$ in (8 cm)
Distribution	Europe, Central Asia, Middle East, North Africa

Above A two-striped grasshopper makes a spectacular leap into the air to escape a predator. Its jump is powered by the large muscles in its back legs.

Grasshoppers and relatives

Above A flower mantis seizes a butterfly with its spiny front legs in a Costa Rican rainforest.

While not all the insects in this chapter are closely related, most share certain features. Many are strong-jawed with mobile heads, and most have large hind wings. This group includes some of the most ancient of all insects, such as the cockroaches.

Familiar pests

Some of these insects are familiar, but unwelcome guests in our homes. Cockroaches, for example, are a common indoor pest, although most live outdoors. Earwigs, which are found in every garden, are also considered pests, since many feed on plants. Others in this group are welcome garden visitors because they catch other pests.

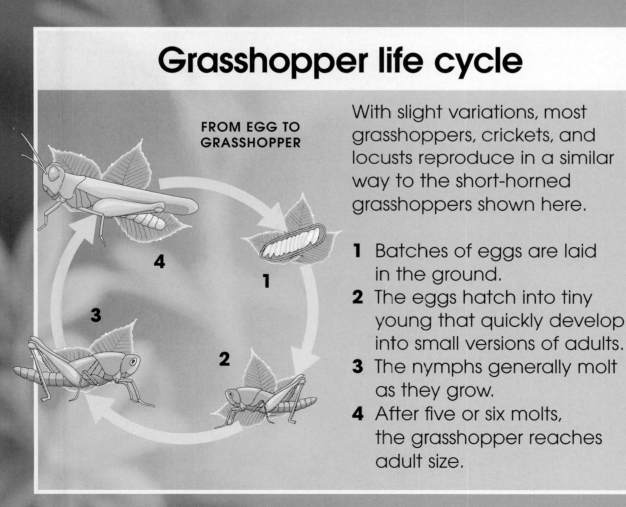

Grasshopper life cycle

FROM EGG TO GRASSHOPPER

With slight variations, most grasshoppers, crickets, and locusts reproduce in a similar way to the short-horned grasshoppers shown here.

1 Batches of eggs are laid in the ground.
2 The eggs hatch into tiny young that quickly develop into small versions of adults.
3 The nymphs generally molt as they grow.
4 After five or six molts, the grasshopper reaches adult size.

Another feature of several of these insects is their ability to conceal themselves by looking like something else. Among the most extraordinary are stick insects, which look like dry twigs, and leaf insects, which resemble leaves. Grasshoppers and crickets are often colored to blend in with their surroundings, and some mantids look like flowers. Termites are very different. They live in huge colonies in nests made on or under the ground, in trees, or in wood.

Earwigs and cockroaches

Cockroaches are one of the most ancient of insect groups and date back more than 350 million years. They adapt easily to many different habitats and thrive everywhere from mountains to rainforests, although they are most common in tropical areas. Despite their bad reputation, only a few species are indoor pests. Earwigs are found in every garden. Many kinds are considered pests, since they feed on plants and flowers. They have flattened bodies, allowing them to crawl into a variety of hiding places.

Long-horned earwig

Family	Labiduridae
Length	Up to 1 1/8 in (2.5 cm)
Number of species	75
Distribution	Worldwide, mainly tropics

Common earwig

An extremely common insect, this earwig has short wings, a long shiny body and forked tail. It eats almost any kind of plant. The female lays her eggs in late winter, usually in a nest under a stone or log. Unusually for an insect, she stays near her eggs to protect them and licks them regularly to keep them clean. Once the young hatch, she continues to look after them and bring them food until can fend for themselves.

Family	Forficulidae
Latin name	Forficula auricularia
Length	1/2 in (1.3 cm)
Distribution	North America and Europe

Common earwig with eggs and young

Long-horned earwigs

This family of earwigs are also known as striped earwigs because of the dark markings on the body. Long-horned earwigs stay hidden during the day and come out at night to hunt other insects. If attacked, they squirt out a bad-smelling liquid from special glands in the abdomen. They have large, semicircular back wings that have to be folded many times to fit under the smaller, leathery front wings.

American cockroach

This insect probably came from Africa originally, but has now spread all over the world. It generally stays hidden during the day and comes out at night to feed on anything it can find. It is attracted to sweet things but will also eat paper, hair, cloth, and almost any rotting matter. The female lays her eggs into a purse-shaped container that is attached to her body. She leaves this egg case in a dark safe place before the eggs hatch. These long-lived cockroaches can live for up to four years and a female may lay as many as 1,000 eggs in her lifetime.

Family	Blattidae
Latin name	*Periplaneta americana*
Length	Up to 2 in (5 cm)
Distribution	Worldwide

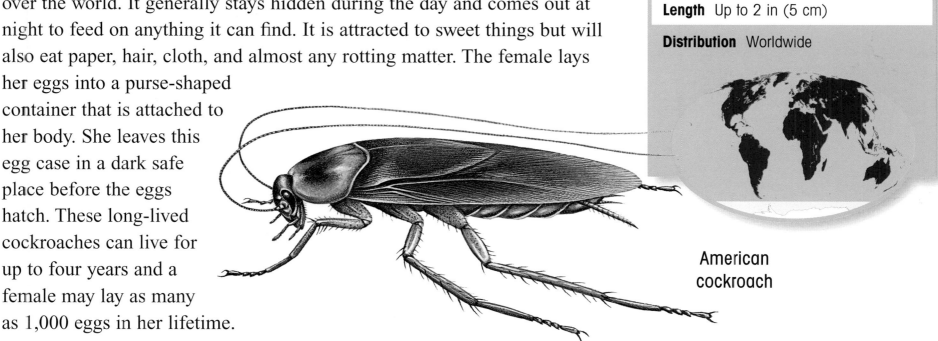

American cockroach

German cockroach

Like the American cockroach, this insect probably came from Africa originally, but is now found all over the world. It lives anywhere it can find food, and eats anything and everything. Like all cockroaches, it is a fast runner. Its flattened body is ideally shaped for squeezing into cracks and under floorboards.

Family	Blatellidae
Latin name	*Blatella germanica*
Length	Up to 7/8 in (2 cm)
Distribution	Worldwide

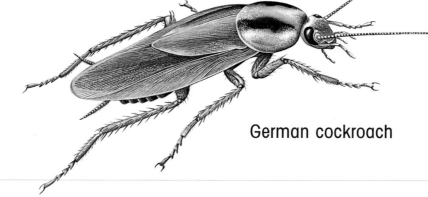

German cockroach

Madagascar hissing cockroach

When alarmed, this large, wingless cockroach makes a loud hissing sound through breathing holes in its abdomen. Males also hiss during battles with rivals. Like most cockroach species, this insect is not an indoor pest but lives in forests where it feeds mostly on leaves and fruit. These insects breed well in captivity and are kept in laboratories and even as pets.

Family	Blaberidae
Latin name	*Gromphadorhina portentosa*
Length	3 in (7.5 cm)
Distribution	Madagascar

Madagascar hissing cockroach

Mantids

Flower mantis

Mantids are among the fiercest predators in the insect world and are well known for their hunting techniques. There are about 1,800 species, the majority of which live in tropical areas. Most mantids have long, slender bodies and triangular heads. They are equipped with long front legs, which they extend at lightning speed to grasp their prey— they rarely miss. These legs have large muscles and are much more powerful than the other legs. A mantid's mouthparts are very strong and able to crunch through the toughest insect prey.

Flower mantises

Camouflage is an important part of the mantids' hunting technique. It helps them stay hidden as they lie in wait for their prey to come close enough to catch. Most mantids are green or brown, but flower mantises are colored to match the flowers on which they perch. This helps them stay hidden from both their prey and their enemies.

Family	Mantidae
Length	Up to 6 in (15 cm)
Number of species	1,400
Distribution	North America, Europe, Asia

Praying mantis

This insect gets its name from its habit of sitting with its front legs folded like a person at prayer. These legs, the mantis's main hunting tools, are lined with sharp spines, which help the mantis to grip its struggling prey as it feeds. Female are usually larger than males, and often attack or even eat males during mating. The male has to get away quickly if he is to escape his mate's deadly embrace.

Praying mantis

Family	Mantidae
Latin name	*Mantis religiosa*
Length	2$\frac{1}{2}$ in (6 cm)
Distribution	North America, Europe, Asia

Carolina mantis

Carolina mantis

The Carolina mantis is usually seen in gardens and fields, perched on flowers or small bushes and other plants. It preys on insects such as butterflies, moths, flies, wasps, and bees. It has a long head and thorax, and its wings are shorter than its abdomen. At the beginning of winter, it lays its eggs in rows on plant stems. They hatch in spring. The young mantids or larvae look like tiny versions of their parents and immediately start hunting small prey.

Family	Mantidae
Latin name	*Stagmomantis carolina*
Length	Up to 2½ in (6 cm)
Distribution	U.S.A., Mexico, Central America

Mediterranean mantis

Pale in color when young, this mantis turns deeper green as it matures. It is similar in appearance to the praying mantis, but has an orange-red spot toward the end of the abdomen. It also has dark spots on the wings, which can be seen when the wings unfold. Like other mantids, this insect's head swivels freely on its neck. It can turn its head to look over its shoulder to follow the movements of its victim.

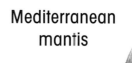

Mediterranean mantis

Family	Mantidae
Latin name	*Iris oratoria*
Length	Up to 2⅝ in (6.5 cm)
Distribution	North America, Europe, Asia

Chinese mantis

Family	Mantidae
Latin name	*Tenodera aridifolia*
Length	4 in (10 cm)
Distribution	China; introduced into North America

Chinese mantis

The Chinese mantis was introduced into North America at the end of the 19th century to help control insect pests. It is now the largest, most common mantis in North America. Although insects are its main food, it can also catch small animals such as lizards and frogs. Coloration varies from brown to green. There is a green stripe on the wings.

Termites

Termites are social insects like some bees, ants, and wasps, although they are not related. They live in huge colonies in nests made in wood, soil, trees, or in specially built mounds. Small and soft-bodied, termites depend on their nests for shelter; they can die within a few hours when exposed to open air. The majority of termites in a colony are blind, wingless workers that build the nest and tend the queen and larvae. The queen is many times bigger than other termites and her sole purpose is to lay eggs. She has her own chamber in the nest, where she lives with her mate. At certain times of year, special termites with wings and eyes fly out of the colony to set up new colonies. Termites feed on different types of plant material.

Family	Termitidae
Length	Up to 2½ in (6 cm)
Number of species	Over 1,800
Distribution	Mainly in South America, Asia, and Australia

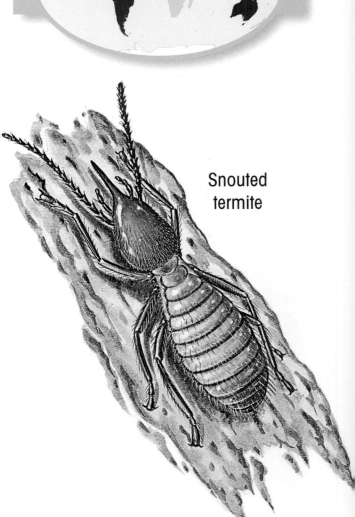

Snouted termite

Subterranean termites

Family	Rhinotermitidae
Length	Up to ³⁄₈ in (1 cm)
Number of species	300
Distribution	Worldwide, excluding polar regions

As their name suggests, these termites live in nests that are at least partially underground. They eat the wood of rotting trees and roots and also do serious damage to wooden buildings. Colonies are huge, numbering millions of insects. Queen subterranean termites are capable of laying over 100 eggs a day.

Subterranean termite

Snouted termites

Most termite colonies have special soldier termites to defend them against enemies such as ants, which may attack their nests. The soldiers of this group of termites have long snouts, which they use to spray sticky bad-smelling fluid at ants and other enemies.

Drywood termites

These termites usually nest in wood above the ground and often attack the wood of buildings, furniture, and even stored timber. Special microscopic organisms in their gut help them digest this tough diet. Specialized soldier termites have larger heads and jaws than others of their species and it is their job to defend the colony against enemies.

Family Kalotermitidae

Length $^3/_8$– $^1/_2$ in (1–1.3 cm)

Number of species Over 400

Distribution Worldwide, excluding polar regions

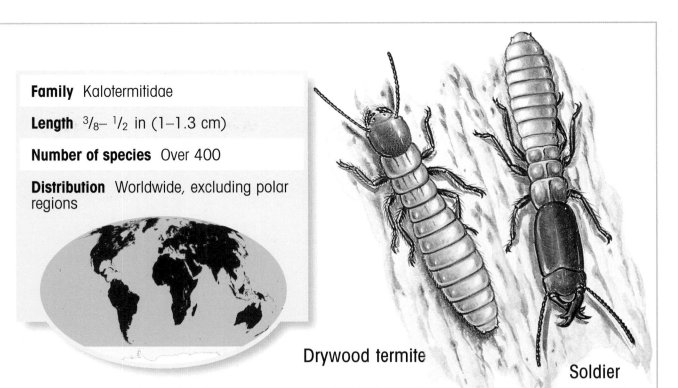

Drywood termite

Soldier

Fungus-growing termite

The termites of this species build some of the largest and most complex nests of any insect. Much of the nest is underground, but above it is a huge chimney rising 25 ft (7.6 m) or more into the air. There are many chambers inside the nest including special "gardens" where fungi are grown by the workers for use as food.

Family Termitidae

Latin name *Macrotermes bellicosus*

Length $^3/_8$ in (1 cm)

Distribution Africa

Fungus-growing termite

Formosan termite

Originally from China, this termite has spread to North America where it is a very serious pest that can cause significant economic problems. One colony may contain several million insects and because of the huge numbers these termites can cause severe structural damage. Soldiers of this termite species have an oval head and curving jaws. They can spray a sticky fluid against enemies.

Formosan termite

Family Rhinotermitidae

Latin name *Coptotermes formosanus*

Length Up to $^5/_8$ in (1.5 cm)

Distribution North America, China

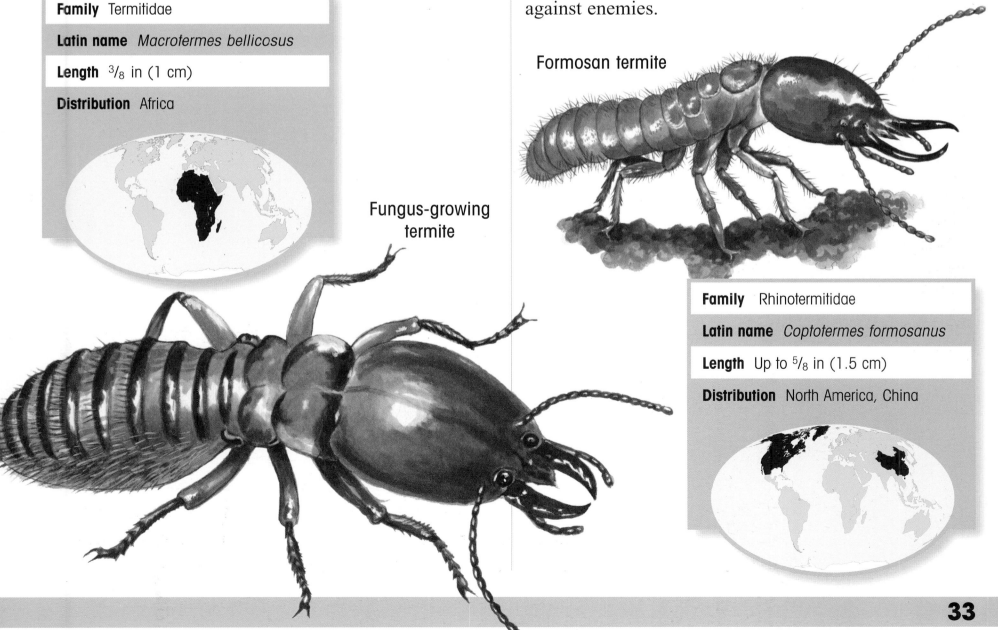

Short-horned grass- hoppers and locusts

There are two main groups of grasshopper: short-horned and long-horned. The short-horned grasshoppers, which include locusts, are named for their short antennae— usually about half the body length. They are well known for their rasping calls, which they make by rubbing the special rough patches on the back wings against the front wings. All grasshoppers have large heads and big eyes, and their sight and hearing are excellent. Most have two pairs of wings. The narrow front pair are used only as covers for the back wings. The broader back wings can be folded away under the front wings.

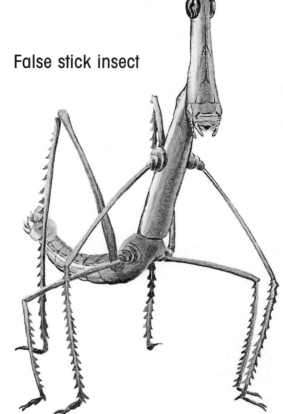

False stick insect

Family	Proscopiidae
Length	Up to 6½ in (16.5 cm)
Number of species	130
Distribution	South America

Desert locust

Among the most damaging of all insects, the desert locust has two very different lifestyles. When there is plenty of food the insects live and feed alone. But from time to time when there is a drought and food is hard to find the locusts gather in huge swarms that may contain as many as 50 billion insects. The locusts swoop down onto crops and feed until there is scarcely a leaf left.

Desert locust

Family	Acrididae
Latin name	*Schistocerca gregaria*
Length	Up to 2½ in (6 cm)
Distribution	Africa, Middle East, Asia

False stick insects

These strange-looking creatures are actually grasshoppers, not stick insects. But, like stick insects, they escape enemies by looking like inedible sticks. They live in trees, bushes, and low-growing plants in tropical rainforests and scrub.

Spur-throated grasshoppers

Despite their large wings, these grasshoppers are not very strong fliers. They spend much of their lives on the ground among grass and other plants. They escape danger by leaping into the air and flying a short distance before settling down again. The jump, which may be a distance of more than 200 times the body length of the grasshopper, is powered by the large muscles in its back legs. As it reaches the height of its jump, it may spread its wings to reveal their bright colors.

Family	Acrididae (Melanoplinae)
Length	Up to 2³/₄ in (7 cm)
Number of species	9,000
Distribution	Temperate and tropical regions worldwide

Spur-throated grasshopper

Blue-winged grasshopper

The mottled coloration of this grasshopper makes it hard to see on the ground when its wings are folded. But when flying up to escape danger, it reveals a flash of brilliant blue on the hind wings, which further startles any enemies. Like all short-horned grasshoppers, it lays its eggs on the ground. The tiny young quickly develop into small versions of the adult insects.

Family	Acrididae
Latin name	*Oedipoda caerulescens*
Length	Up to 1¹/₄ in (3 cm)
Distribution	Europe

Blue-winged grasshopper

Pygmy grasshoppers

Also known as groundhoppers or grouse locusts, these little grasshoppers are mostly brown in color. Their distinguishing feature is the long pronotum, a kind of shield made from part of the top of the thorax, that extends over most of the body. In some species the front wings are just small scales. These grasshoppers generally live near ponds and streams and feed on algae and moss.

Pygmy grasshopper

Family	Tetrigidae
Length	Up to ⁷/₈ in (2 cm)
Number of species	850
Distribution	Temperate and tropical regions worldwide

Long-horned grasshoppers

Insects of this group, which includes katydids and bush-crickets, can grow up to a length of 3 in (7.5 cm) and have very long antennae—hence their common name. Found worldwide, they are most common in tropical areas. Long-horned grasshoppers make their shrill call in a different way from their short-horned relatives. On one wing there is a scraper and on the other a ridged vein. To make its song, the grasshopper lifts its wings and rubs them together. Its hearing organs are on its front legs.

Northern katydid

Family	Tettigoniidae
Latin name	Pterophylla camellifolia
Length	Up to 2³⁄₈ in (5.5 cm)
Distribution	Eastern U.S.A.

Meadow katydids

Family	Tettigoniidae (Conocephalinae)
Length	Up to 3 in (7.5 cm)
Number of species	1,000
Distribution	Worldwide

Also known as coneheaded katydids, these insects have a long cone-shaped head and large jaws. They feed on the seed heads of grasses and many generally only come out at night. Their front wings are long and narrow and they are strong fliers. These insects sometimes hide in clumps of grass. They crawl in head-first and look much like another blade of grass.

Meadow katydid

Northern katydid

This grasshopper gets its name from the male's song, which is said to sound like "katy-did," and sometimes "katy-didn't." Its bright green wings are marked with leaflike veins that help it hide as it perches among plants. The female has a knifelike ovipositor (egg-laying tube). She uses this to insert her eggs into slots that she cuts in the stems of plants. Eggs are usually laid in the fall and hatch the following spring.

Oak bush-cricket

Brazilian false-leaf katydid

Many grasshoppers protect themselves from enemies by looking like something else. This Brazilian species looks amazingly like a dead leaf as it perches among the leaf litter on the forest floor. The mottled coloration and veinlike markings of the front wings help the insect merge into its surroundings. But if startled it leaps up, flashing the brightly colored eye spots on its back wings to confuse its attacker.

Family	Tettigoniidae
Latin name	*Meconema thalassinum*
Length	Up to 7/8 in (2 cm)
Distribution	North America, Europe

Oak bush-cricket

This bush-cricket has been introduced from its native Europe into North America. Males do not sing but do make a drumming sound by tapping on leaves with their hind legs. Because of this, these insects are sometimes known as drumming katydids. They generally live on oak trees and the female lays her eggs under the bark.

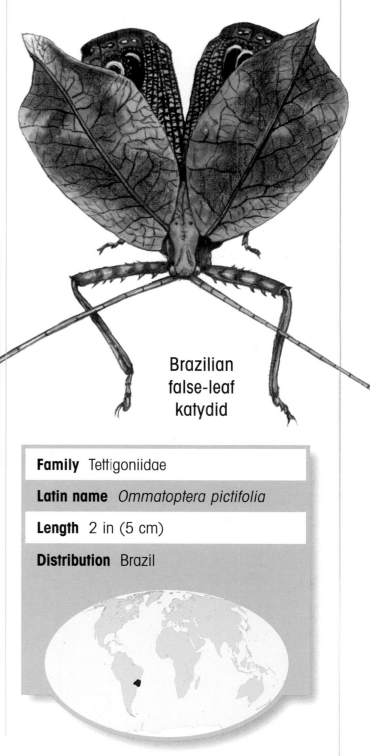

Great green bush-cricket

These insects usually come out at dusk and are active through the night. They feed on plants, but also catch and eat small insects. They live among bushes and shrubs, and are often hard to see. Males sing their rattling courtship song in the late afternoon and evening.

Family	Tettigoniidae
Latin name	*Tettigonia viridissima*
Length	Up to 2³/₈ in (5.5 cm)
Distribution	Europe

Brazilian false-leaf katydid

Family	Tettigoniidae
Latin name	*Ommatoptera pictifolia*
Length	2 in (5 cm)
Distribution	Brazil

Great green bush-cricket

Crickets

Most true crickets "sing" by rubbing together the specially ridged and thickened areas of their front wings to make a high-pitched sound. Their hearing organs are on the base of the front legs. Crickets are usually colored green, black, or brown and have broad bodies, long antennae, and well-developed feelers at the end of the abdomen.

Camel cricket

Camel crickets

The humped back of these crickets makes them easy to spot and gives them their common name. They also have very long legs and long antennae. Most are wingless and therefore cannot "sing" like other crickets, but some species can make sounds by rubbing the inside of the back leg against the body. They generally live in dark basements or caves or under piles of wood. Their other common name is cave cricket.

House cricket

Family	Gryllidae
Latin name	*Acheta domestica*
Length	$^5/_8$–$^7/_8$ in (1.5–2 cm)
Distribution	Worldwide

This cricket usually lives indoors where, as well as food scraps, it eats clothing and other items. It usually stays hidden during the day and comes out at night to find food. Its usual song is a three-note chirp, but courting males sing continuously. Females lay their eggs in any little crack or hole indoors at any time of year.

Family	Rhaphidophoridae
Length	Up to 2 in (5 cm)
Number of species	About 350
Distribution	Worldwide

House cricket

Field cricket

This cricket spends most of its time outside, hiding among plants on the ground, but will go into houses in the winter for warmth. It eats plant matter, including seedlings, and sometimes damages crops. However, the field cricket also feeds on the eggs and larvae of some other pest insects. The female uses her pointed egg-laying tube to insert her eggs into the earth.

Family	Gryllidae
Latin name	*Gryllus pennsylvanicus*
Length	$5/8$–$1\,1/8$ in (1.5–2.5 cm)
Distribution	North America

Field cricket

Mole crickets

Like tiny moles, these crickets live under the ground, where they burrow with their large spadelike front legs. A covering of fine hairs protects the insect's body from the soil. Plant roots are the mole crickets' main food, and they often damage crops and trees. They also catch and eat worms and larvae. The females lay their eggs in an underground tunnel.

Family	Gryllotalpidae
Length	About $7/8$ in (2 cm)
Number of species	60
Distribution	Worldwide

Mole cricket

Snowy tree cricket

Snowy tree cricket

This cricket is also known as the thermometer cricket. It is said that you can find out the Fahrenheit temperature by counting the number of chirps it makes in 13 seconds and then adding 40. It usually lives in woodlands and forests and feeds on other insects, such as aphids and caterpillars. The female lays her eggs in trees, inserting them into the bark with her sharp egg-laying tube. She usually does this in early winter and the young emerge in spring.

Family	Gryllidae
Latin name	*Oecanthus fultoni*
Length	$5/8$ in (1.5 cm)
Distribution	North America

Termite nests

Many insects have short lives and do not need to make homes. However, some families of insects do make elaborate shelters in which huge colonies live. Termite nests may house a million or more individuals. The purpose of the nest is to provide protection from enemies and a dark, warm, humid environment in which to live. Termites depend on this shelter and cannot survive exposure to the open air for more than a few hours. Their nests may be made in trees, on the ground, or underground.

Below The huge tower of a termite nest helps to keep the insects' living quarters below well ventilated. This termite tower is in the Australian Tanami Desert.

Termite towers

The most dramatic insect nests are those made by some species of termite in Africa. These nests reach a height of 25 ft (7.6 m) and are made of mud which, when mixed with saliva from the worker termites, hardens like concrete when it dries.

The main part of the nest is concealed underground and contains chambers for larvae and food storage. The queen termite lives in a special cell, where she is tended by workers. This type of termite also grows special fungus, which the insects eat and feed to their young, and these "fungus gardens" are also below ground. Foraging tunnels lead out from the nest to the surface so that the termites can get in and out.

Above Mushroom-shaped termite mounds like this one in Cameroon are designed to resist the heavy rainfall that can occur in rainforest regions.

40

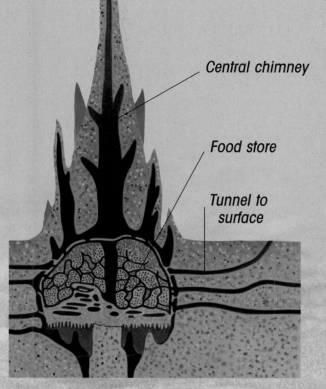

Central chimney

Food store

Tunnel to surface

Above Chambers inside the nest are used to store food and for rearing termite larvae. The queen termite has her own chamber.

Ventilation

The great chimney of the nest works like a ventilation shaft and helps to keep conditions constant inside the structure. Air from inside the nest rises up to the central part of the spire and into the side chimneys, which have thinner walls than the rest of the nest. The chimneys allow carbon dioxide to pass out and oxygen to pass into the nest. The temperature inside remains virtually the same from day to day, even though outside it may change dramatically.

Tree nests

Some termites make their nests around tree branches. The nest is made from little pieces of wood and termite saliva. Inside is a maze of passages, with the queen termite's cell at the center. Covered passageways lead from the termite nest down the trunk and branches. These protect the termites as they travel to and from the nest. If a passageway is damaged it must be quickly repaired by the workers of the termite colony.

Above Tree nests similar to this one are very common in the rainforests of Brazil. They help the termites stay out of the reach of predators.

Leaf insects and stick insects

This group of insects are best known for their ability to stay camouflaged by looking like leaves or twigs. There are around 3,000 species in all, and most live in tropical regions, where they feed on leaves and other plant materials. They are generally active at night. The females of most species lay their eggs on the ground. The eggs hatch into tiny versions of their parents. As they grow they molt a number of times until they reach adult size.

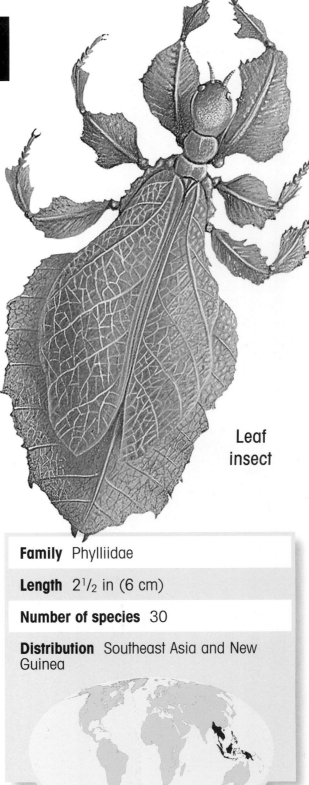

Leaf insect

Family	Phylliidae
Length	2¹/₂ in (6 cm)
Number of species	30
Distribution	Southeast Asia and New Guinea

Stick insects

Family	Phasmatidae
Length	Up to 6 in (15 cm)
Number of species	750
Distribution	Tropical and subtropical regions

With their slender green or brown bodies, stick insects look so like leafless twigs that they are hard for birds and other predators to see. During the day they cling to plants, with only their long, thin legs swaying gently. At night, stick insects move around, feeding on leaves. Some stick insects can change color according to the leaves among which they live. Some stick insects are also known as walking sticks.

Leaf insects

These amazing insects are shaped just like the leaves they live on, complete with veins. Even the legs are leaflike and the insects' eggs look like the seeds of the plant. Some leaf insects have ragged edges to their body resembling bite marks. As they walk, leaf insects often sway slightly like leaves in the breeze. Only the males can fly.

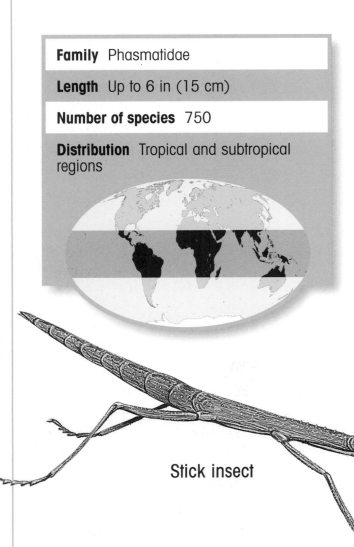

Stick insect

Timemas

These little insects are mostly wingless. They live on trees and shrubs where they feed on leaves. Typically a timema has a stubby, leaflike body with long antennae and a pair of small appendages at the end of the body. Timemas cannot fly but do run quickly to escape from danger. The eggs, laid on the ground at the beginning of winter, hatch in spring.

Spiny leaf insect

Timema

Titan stick insect

Female titans are among Australia's largest insects, but males are only about half their size. Like all stick insects, titans rely on camouflage to protect them from enemies and they sit with their legs held out in front of them to look as sticklike as possible. If disturbed, a titan may fly off flashing the purple underside of its wigs to startle its attacker. Titans usually live on eucalyptus and acacia trees, and feed on their leaves. They lay their eggs on the ground among dead leaves.

Spiny leaf insect

These curious insects are popular pets in Australia. The female has a large body but very small wings and so cannot fly. Males are smaller and more slender, and have longer wings with which they can fly. The female usually lays her eggs on the ground under her feeding tree. Each egg has a small knob on it that ants like to eat. The ants take the eggs to their nests, eat the knobs, and leave the eggs in the nest, safe from other predators. When the young hatch they climb out of the ant nest and up into a tree to find leaves to eat.

Titan stick insect

Stoneflies, barklice, and webspinners

These are all separate insect groups. Barklice are not lice at all but a completely different group called psocids. This group also includes booklice, which are wingless insects often found in houses. They often feed on the glue of bookbindings, causing considerable damage. Webspinners live in large colonies in webs. Stoneflies are not true flies but an ancient group of soft-bodied insects, which spend most of their time resting on stones. Also included here are rock crawlers, a small group of termite-like insects that can survive low temperatures.

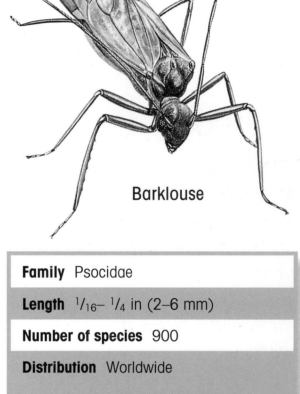

Barklouse

Family	Psocidae
Length	$^1/_{16}$– $^1/_4$ in (2–6 mm)
Number of species	900
Distribution	Worldwide

Common stoneflies

Adult stoneflies have a short life lasting only two to three weeks and most do not feed. The male attracts females by drumming on a hard surface with the tip of its abdomen. The female may drum back. She lays her eggs in streams. Once hatched, the larvae (or nymphs) live in the water, feeding on plants or insects. The nymphs can take in oxygen through their body surface but they also have gills, which help them to breathe under water. As they grow, the nymphs molt until they make their final molt into adult form and leave the water.

Barklice

A typical barklouse is a small insect with a large head and long antennae. Most barklice live on or under the bark of trees and bushes. They feed on lichen and algae, which they chew with their large jaws. Many kinds are wingless, but others have fully developed wings and can fly. When at rest, barklice hold their wings up above the body.

Family	Perlidae
Length	$^3/_8$–$1^1/_2$ in (1–4 cm)
Number of species	400
Distribution	Worldwide, excluding southern Asia and Australia

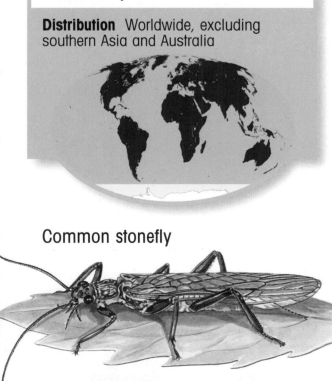

Common stonefly

Giant stonefly

These are the largest of the stoneflies and, although they have a wingspan of up to 3 in (8 cm), they are not strong fliers. The hind wings have fanlike edges. They are generally active at night and usually live on rocks near water. The adults do not feed but the young eat algae. The eggs are laid in water and sink to the bottom. Once hatched, the young may spend a year or more as water-living nymphs before crawling out to molt into their adult form.

Family Pteronarcidae

Latin name *Pteronarcys californica*

Length 1 1/4–1 1/2 in (3–4 cm)

Distribution North America

Giant stonefly

Webspinners

Little is known about these insects and, although only about 170 species have been named, scientists believe there may be 2,000 or more different kinds. These insects live in colonies and spin silk that they make into tunnels on bark or stones. They can then move through these protective runways between their nest and food supplies, such as rotting leaves, lichen, and moss. Only females and young feed. Males are short-lived and do not eat.

Webspinner

Order Embioptera

Length 1/8– 3/8 in (3–10 mm)

Number of species 170

Distribution Tropical and subtropical regions worldwide

Order Grylloblattodea

Length 5/8–1 1/4 in (1.5–3 cm)

Number of species 25

Distribution Mountains in Asia and North America

Rock crawler

Rock crawlers

Also known as ice crawlers, these rare insects are found only high on mountains in scattered locations. Small and wingless, they prefer cool, wet places and live on the ground under stones or among rotting leaves. Rock crawlers prey on other insects and, in icy areas, they also feed on insects that have died from cold. They have thin, flattened bodies covered with fine hairs. They were first discovered in 1914 in the Canadian Rockies.

Below Bee assassin bugs, such as this Costa Rican species, are named for their habit of waiting on flowers to prey on visiting bees.

Bugs, lice, and thrips

Above This stinkbug has just caught a beetle and is preparing to feast on its prey.

Although the name bug is often used for insects in general, it actually describes a particular order of insects—the Hemiptera. This group includes a wide variety of species such as assassin bugs, stinkbugs, water boatmen, and cicadas, as well as familiar plant pests such as aphids. Bugs vary in size from tiny creatures less than a centimeter long to large insects measuring up to $4^1/_2$ in (11 cm) long.

Main features

The most important feature of a bug is its mouthparts. These are specialized to pierce a food source and suck up the liquid inside. Many bugs feed on plant juices but some, such as the giant water bug, hunt other creatures. A few types—for example, bedbugs, are parasites; they live on other creatures, including humans and other mammals, and feed on their blood.

Lice and thrips

Lice are small, wingless insects that live as parasites on birds and mammals. Plant-eating thrips are related to lice, but they are not parasites. They live on bark and flowers, and feed on plant juices.

Bug life cycle

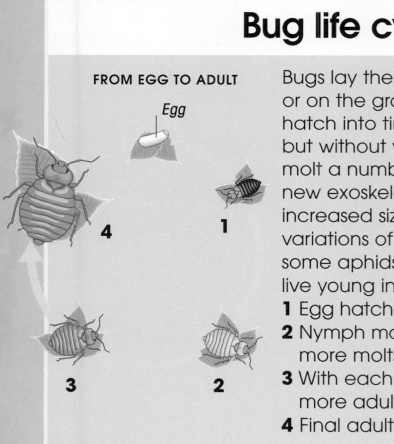

FROM EGG TO ADULT

Egg

4 1

3 2

Bugs lay their eggs on or inside plants or on the ground. Typically, the eggs hatch into tiny versions of their parents, but without wings. As they grow, they molt a number of times and grow a new exoskeleton that fits their increased size. There are many variations of this basic pattern and some aphids and mealybugs produce live young instead of laying eggs.

1 Egg hatches into tiny wingless nymph.
2 Nymph makes its first molt. Up to five more molts may follow.
3 With each molt the nymph becomes more adultlike in appearance.
4 Final adult stage.

Lice, zorapterans, and thrips

There are two main types of lice: sucking lice and chewing lice and many can have a serious effect on the health of their hosts. Very little is known about zorapterans, a small group of insects, which were only discovered in 1913. Some experts think they may be related to cockroaches. Thrips are a larger group—including as many as 5,000 species. They are related to lice and some are pests of particular plants and may damage crops.

Feather louse

Family	Philopteridae
Length	$\frac{1}{16}$ in (2 mm)
Number of species	1,500
Distribution	Worldwide

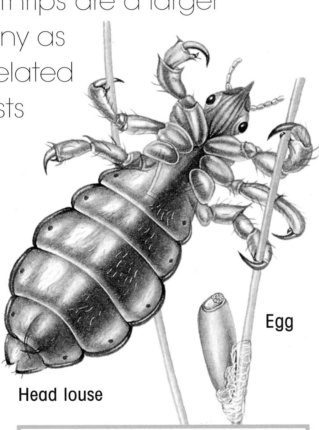

Egg

Head louse

Head louse

The head louse lives on human heads, feeding on blood. It secures itself on the head by holding onto hairs with its strong legs and claws. It cannot fly or even jump, so can only transfer from person to person when their heads are in close contact. The female lays her eggs on the host's head, gluing them to hairs with a cementlike substance that she produces with her eggs. Once it hatches, the young louse, called a nymph, starts to feed on blood. It molts three times before it attains adult size.

Family	Pediculidae
Latin name	*Pediculis humanus capitis*
Length	$\frac{1}{8}$ in (3 mm)
Distribution	Worldwide

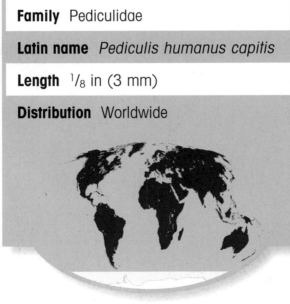

Feather lice

Feather lice belong to the group of chewing lice and live on a wide range of birds. They have two claws on each leg, which they use to cling on to their host's feathers. They feed by biting off pieces of feather and dead skin with their strong jaws. Females lay up to 100 eggs, which they fix to the feathers of the host with a gluey substance that they make in their own bodies.

Chicken body louse

This louse lives on chickens and other domestic fowl such as turkeys and guineafowl. It feeds on bits of skin and feathers and can cause great irritation to the host bird. These lice can have a commercial impact as the health of an infested bird declines and it loses weight and lays fewer eggs.

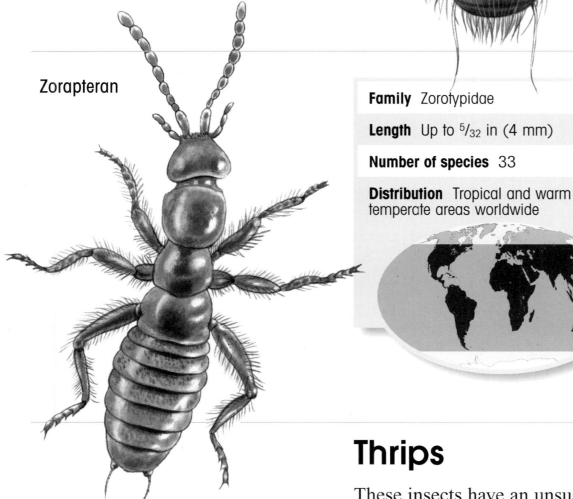

Family	Menoponidae
Latin name	*Menacanthus stramineus*
Length	$1/8$ in (3 mm)
Distribution	Worldwide

Chicken body louse

Zorapteran

Family	Zorotypidae
Length	Up to $5/32$ in (4 mm)
Number of species	33
Distribution	Tropical and warm temperate areas worldwide

Zorapterans

Tiny, soft-bodied zorapterans live in groups on bark, logs, or rotting wood, but they feed mostly on fungus. They are sometimes found in termite nests, possibly attracted by the termites' fungus gardens. There are winged and wingless forms, but winged males are rare. The eggs hatch into larvae, which molt four or five times as they grow to adult size.

Thrips

These insects have an unsual feeding method; only the left jaw, or mandible, is developed and forms a feeding tube that the thrip uses to puncture leaves or flowers and suck out the contents. Some thrips feed on fungus in the same way and others eat small creatures such as mites. In some species there are no males and the female can breed rapidly without mating, producing only females.

Family	Thripidae
Length	Up to $5/8$ in (1.5 cm)
Number of species	1,700
Distribution	Worldwide, mostly in tropical areas

Thrip

True bugs

This amazingly varied order of insects, the Hemiptera, includes about 90,000 known species. All have sucking mouthparts, and unlike other bugs, these insects can swing their beaklike feeding apparatus forward so enabling them to take advantage of a greater range of foods. All have stink glands to warn off enemies and many are brightly colored.

Plantbugs

The biggest family of true bugs, plantbugs live all over the world in almost every kind of habitat. Most feed on leaves, seeds, and fruit, and some are serious pests of important food crops such as alfalfa, cotton, and tea. Other plantbugs are more welcome to farmers since they feed on insects such as aphids, which are also pests. Plantbugs have delicate, often brightly colored bodies. Female plantbugs use their sharp-tipped ovipositor (egg-laying tube) to insert their eggs into plant stems.

Family	Miridae
Length	$^1/_{16}$–$^5/_8$ in (0.2–1.5 cm)
Number of species	10,000
Distribution	Worldwide

Plantbug

Stinkbugs

These bugs live all over the world but are most common in tropical areas. They get their name from the particularly foul-smelling liquid that they squirt at any creature that tries to attack them. The liquid comes from glands on the underside of the body. The stinkbug's mouthparts are inside its beaklike snout. It uses these to pierce the surface of a plant to get at the sap inside. Some species of this family are very serious pests of soybeans.

Stinkbug

Family	Pentatomidae
Length	$^5/_{32}$–$^7/_8$ in (4–20 mm)
Number of species	4,500
Distribution	Worldwide

Bedbugs

Bedbugs usually stay hidden during the day, then come out at night to feed on the blood of birds and mammals. They do not live on their host but in its home or nest, and their flattened shape makes it easy for them to hide in crevices. Bedbugs have a somewhat dramatic method of mating. The male has a bladelike penis, which he uses to tear open the female's abdomen so he can insert his sperm.

Family	Cimicidae
Length	Up to $1/4$ in (6 mm)
Number of species	100
Distribution	Worldwide

Bedbug

Shieldbugs

Also known as jewel bugs, many of these insects are brightly colored and among the most beautiful of all bugs. Their main characteristic is that part of the thorax extends to make a shieldlike covering over the wings and body. This makes them look rather like beetles, but the shieldbug's shield is continuous, not divided in the middle like that of a beetle. Shieldbugs feed on plant juices, which they suck out with their mouthparts. A few are serious pests of grain crops in the Middle East and Asia.

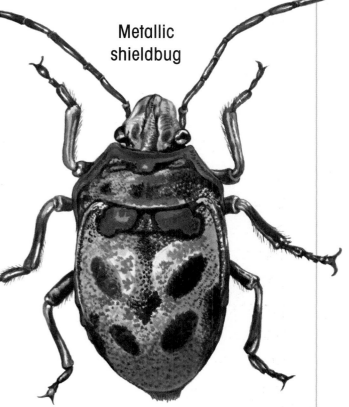

Metallic shieldbug

Assassin bugs

Fierce-looking assassin bugs attack and kill other insects, such as caterpillars, beetles, and bees. Once the bug has grasped its prey, it injects some spit, or saliva, which paralyzes its prey. The bug then sucks up the body juices of its victim. Some assassin bug species also bite large mammals, including humans, to feed on their blood, and a few spread a serious illness called Chaga's disease.

Family	Reduviidae
Length	$7/32$–$1 1/2$ in (0.7–4 cm)
Number of species	6,500
Distribution	Worldwide, especially tropics

Family	Scutelleridae
Length	$3/16$–$7/8$ in (0.5–2 cm)
Number of species	400–500
Distribution	Worldwide

Assassin bug

Water bugs

More than 2,000 different species of true bug live in fresh water—in ponds, streams, and lakes. Some, such as pond skaters and water measurers, are so light that they can run over the water without breaking the surface and rarely even get wet. Others, such as water boatmen, water bugs, and water scorpions, live beneath the surface and hunt for their food in water. They are not able to take oxygen from the water, however, and so have to come to the surface from time to time to breathe air.

Giant water bug

Family	Belastomatidae
Length	Up to 4¼ in (11 cm)
Number of species	150

Distribution Worldwide, most common in tropical regions

Water measurers

Family	Hydrometridae
Length	Up to ⅞ in (2 cm)
Number of species	119

Distribution Worldwide, most common in tropical regions

The water measurer's feet are covered with waterproof hairs, which help it walk on the surface of the water as it looks for food such as mosquito larvae. It tends to sit and wait for its victims to come close rather than chasing them, and often spears prey below the surface with its long slender head.

Giant water bugs

Giant water bugs are the largest members of the bug group. Strong swimmers, they paddle with their back and middle legs and use their powerful front legs for catching prey such as fish and frogs. In some species, the females lay their eggs on plants, but in others, she glues her eggs onto the back of a male and he carries them until they hatch. In some parts of the world, these insects are eaten by people and are considered a delicacy.

Water measurer

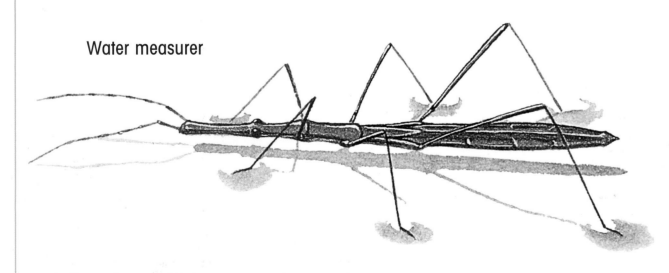

Water boatmen

Water boatman

Unlike other water bugs, these soft-bodied insects are not predators but feed on tiny plants and algae. They collect their food with their front legs and use the middle and oarlike back legs for swimming. When they go underwater, they often make a bubble of air that surrounds the body. These insects are common and lay large numbers of eggs. These are harvested by humans for food in some areas.

Family	Corixidae
Length	Up to $^5/_8$ in (1.5 cm)
Number of species	Over 600
Distribution	Worldwide

Backswimmer

Water scorpions

These insects are not scorpions at all, but a type of bug. They have a long breathing tube at the end of the body, which they use like a snorkel. By holding the breathing tube at the water surface, the bug can hang head down in the water while it waits for passing prey. When a likely victim comes near, the water scorpion seizes it in its powerful front legs and attacks with its beaklike mouthparts. It can even give humans a painful bite.

Family	Notonectidae
Length	Up to $^5/_8$ in (1.5 cm)
Number of species	340
Distribution	Worldwide

Water scorpion

Family	Nepidae
Length	Up to 2 in (5 cm)
Number of species	230
Distribution	Worldwide, most common in tropical regions

Backswimmers

As the common name suggests, these insects swim upside down, using their long back legs as oars. They move fast, chasing and catching other insects as well as small creatures such as tadpoles. They seize their prey with their front legs and stab it with their beaks before sucking out the juices from the body.

Staying hidden

Insects are food for all kinds of animals and so they must have ways of defending themselves. For some, the best strategy is to stay well hidden. Some simply tuck themselves under stones or leaves, but others are colored or shaped in a way that helps them to merge into their surroundings. This is called camouflage and makes the insects hard for other creatures to see.

Above You have to look very closely to see the superbly disguised flower mantis preparing to ambush prey on this orchid flower.

Insect mimics

There are several families of insects and spiders that look remarkably like leaves or twigs, and others that are colored like bark or lichen. Some leaflike insects even have irregular edges to their bodies or wings that make them look as if they have been nibbled by caterpillars. Treehopper bugs have pointed extensions on their bodies, which make them look very like thorns as they cling to tree branches, and birds pass them by. Some kinds of praying mantis look amazingly like the petals of flowers. This works in two ways: the flower mantis is not only camouflaged from predators but is also attractive to prey. Its mimicry is so good that it is investigated by flower-feeding insects, which it swiftly traps.

Adapting to change

Like most moths, the peppered moth flies at night. During the day it rests on tree trunks where its speckled coloration helps it to stay hidden from birds. And these moths have shown they can adapt to changing circumstances. In the 1800s when coal dust and other pollution darkened tree trunks in industrial areas, the moths gradually became darker. Now that this kind of pollution is less of a problem, the moths have become lighter in color.

Masters of disguise

Some kinds of caterpillar are very clever at disguise. The geometrid uses the pair of claspers at the end of its body to hold firmly onto its food plant and then stretches itself out so that it looks like another twig.

Caterpillars of swallowtail butterflies look just like bird droppings on a leaf when they first hatch out. But once they grow too big to pass as droppings, they turn bright green so they are camouflaged against the leaves of their food plant.

Right Lanternbugs often live on tree trunks, where their mottled coloration helps to keep them concealed from predators.

Above With its mottled coloration and straight body, this geometrid caterpillar is almost perfectly camouflaged. It is hard to tell it apart from the twigs on this tree.

Cicadas, treehoppers, and leafhoppers

This group of bugs includes a huge and varied range of insects. They range from tiny leafhoppers measuring a fraction of an inch to giant cicadas of up to 8 inches long. Most feed on plants and a few species are serious pests of food crops. Females have a bladelike egg-laying tube (ovipositor) and generally lay their eggs in plant stems.

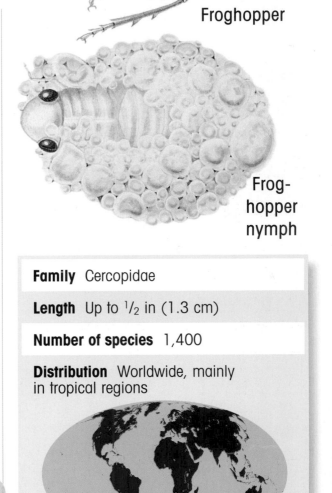

Froghopper

Frog-hopper nymph

Family	Cicadidae
Length	Up to 2½ in (6 cm)
Number of species	At least 2,000
Distribution	Worldwide in temperate and tropical regions

Adult cicada with molted skin

Family	Cercopidae
Length	Up to ½ in (1.3 cm)
Number of species	1,400
Distribution	Worldwide, mainly in tropical regions

Cicadas

These insects are best known for the shrill, almost constant call made by the males. The sound is made by a pair of structures called tymbals, located on the abdomen, which are vibrated by special muscles. Female cicadas usually lay their eggs in slits they make in tree branches.

Froghoppers

Also known as spittlebugs, these little insects hop and crawl about on plants as they suck out sap. They lay their eggs on plant stems and when the nymphs hatch they cover themselves with a substance much like saliva. This comes from glands on the abdomen and mixes with air to form a frothy mass. The froth helps to protect the nymphs and hides them from hungry birds and other predators.

Treehoppers

Most treehoppers have a strangely shaped extension on the thorax which makes them look like a thorn of the plants on which they sit. Many species in this family are brightly colored. Treehoppers feed mostly on sap from trees and other plants. Females lay their eggs in slits in stems and twigs.

Treehopper

Family Membracidae
Length 5/8 in (1.5 cm)
Number of species 2,500
Distribution Worldwide

Fulgorid plant-hoppers

Many of these insects are large and brightly colored and have a large hornlike extension on the head. This may help confuse predators and protect the bug. Fulgorids feed on plant juices, which they suck out with their piercing mouthparts. They are also known as lanternbugs because people used to think their heads glowed in the dark.

Family Fulgoridae
Length Up to 4 in (10 cm)
Number of species 800
Distribution Worldwide, mainly in tropical and subtropical regions

Fulgorid plant-hopper

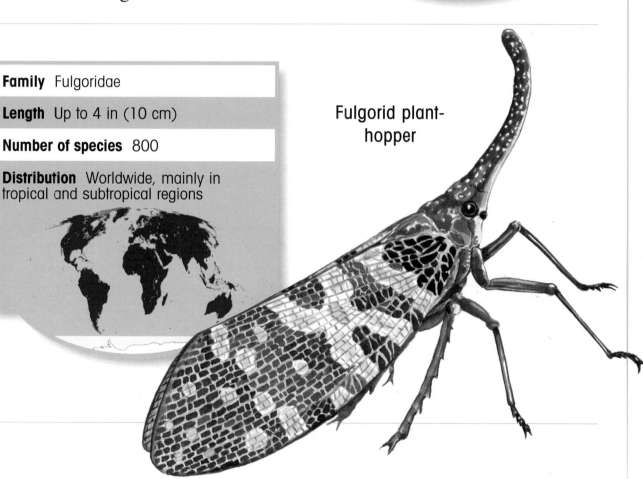

Family Cicadellidae
Length Up to 1 1/4 in (3 cm)
Number of species At least 20,000
Distribution Worldwide

Leafhoppers

This is one of the largest families of insects and new species are regularly discovered. They live on plants in every kind of habitat from deserts to rainforests. Many are brightly colored. As their name suggests, these small insects hop about on plants. They feed on plant juices, which they suck out with their beaklike mouthparts. Many are serious pests of crops such as potatoes and beets. They are a favorite food of many creatures such as birds and lizards, as well as other bugs and spiders. Females lay their eggs in plant stems. When the young hatch, they feed on plants sap, too, and molt five times as they grow to adult size.

Leafhopper

Aphids, scale insects, and relatives

All of these insects are tiny, but they can have a huge impact on plant crops. They all feed on plant juices and, as they occur in large numbers, they can seriously damage plants, leaving them with curled or dying leaves and sometimes spreading diseases from plant to plant. Scale insects, however, have a waxy covering that has proved to be valuable and is used to make lacquers, such as shellac, and dyes.

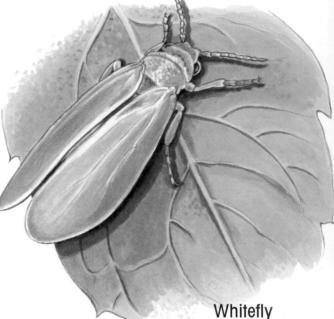
Whitefly

Whiteflies

These tiny insects get their common name from the waxy white powder that covers their wings. They feed on plant sap and, in tropical areas, often do serious damage to food plants such as citrus trees. Whiteflies are less common in temperate areas. Laid on the underside of leaves, the eggs hatch into larvae, which stay in one spot feeding on sap as they grow. They molt four times, then stop feeding for a period as they transform into winged adults.

Family	Aphididae
Length	Up to $3/16$ in (5 mm)
Number of species	At least 4,000
Distribution	Worldwide

Aphids

These small, soft-bodied insects are familiar to gardeners because they feed on sap from plants, causing considerable damage. Most adult females are wingless, but males can fly. Aphids reproduce very quickly, sometimes producing live young instead of laying eggs. Many of the young are eaten by insects such as ladybugs and parasitic wasps. Females also sometimes reproduce without mating. Most aphids excrete a sugary substance called honeydew, which is eaten by other insects.

Aphid

Family	Aleyrodidae
Length	Up to $1/8$ in (3 mm)
Number of species	1,450
Distribution	Worldwide, mainly in tropical regions

Cottony cushion scale

These insects feed on the sap of citrus leaves. In temperate areas, they are often found in greenhouses. The female has an orange, yellow, or brown body, often completely covered by white wax. She has no wings, and her most obvious feature is the large fluted egg case at her rear, containing as many as 1,000 red eggs. The male is winged but much smaller than the female. These insects were such a problem for the orange growers in California in the late 19th century that they imported a ladybug from Australia to eat them.

Cottony cushion scale

Family	Margarodidae
Latin name	*Icerya purchasi*
Length	Up to $3/16$ in (5 mm)
Distribution	Subtropical and tropical regions worldwide

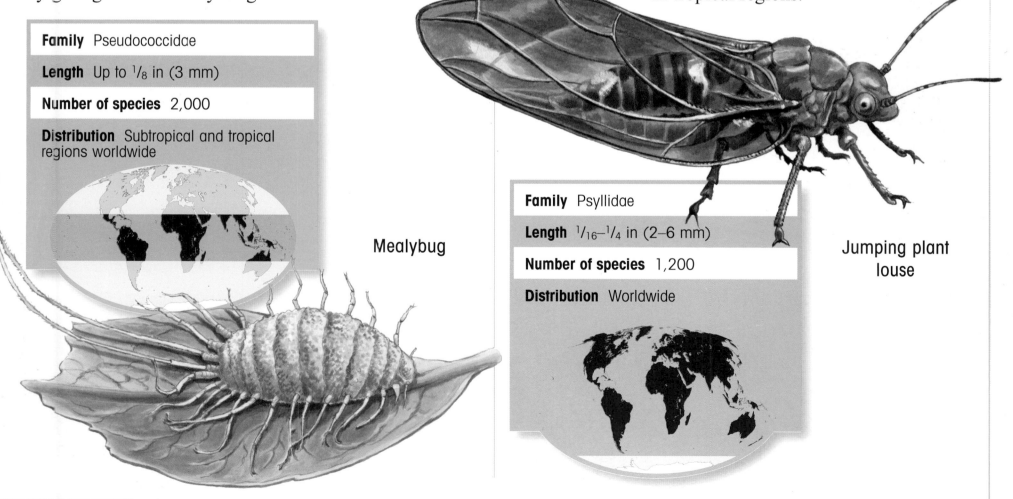

Mealybugs

Tiny soft-bodied insects, mealybugs are covered with a powdery white wax. Females live by sucking juices from the leaves and stems of plants. Although they are most common in tropical and subtropical areas, they also infest greenhouses and can cause damage to plants. Males do not feed and live only long enough to find and mate with females. Mealybugs lay eggs but sometimes increase their numbers even more quickly by giving birth to live young.

Family	Pseudococcidae
Length	Up to $1/8$ in (3 mm)
Number of species	2,000
Distribution	Subtropical and tropical regions worldwide

Mealybug

Jumping plant lice

Also known as psyllids, these insects look like tiny cicadas and can jump as they move around plants feeding on their juices. Some make little clouds of a waxy substance, which may help to hide them from predators. Females lay eggs on leaves, sometimes inserting them into the plant tissue with the aid of an egg-laying tube (or ovipositor). These insects are most common in the southern hemisphere, particularly in tropical regions.

Family	Psyllidae
Length	$1/16$–$1/4$ in (2–6 mm)
Number of species	1,200
Distribution	Worldwide

Jumping plant louse

Above With their gleaming, metallic colors, these leaf beetles are like little jewels. They feed on leaves and flowers, and many species are capable of causing damage to food crops.

Right The male cockchafer beetle has large, fanlike antennae, which help him pick up the scent of females. The antennae can be folded up.

Beetles and weevils

Beetles are the largest of all groups of insects. More than a quarter of a million species are known so far and new ones are discovered every year. Beetles are among the most successful of all living creatures and account for around 40 percent of all insect species.

Secret of success

One of the reasons for the success of this group of insects is that they are so adaptable. Almost every type of habitat from polar lands to rainforests is home to beetles. There is a beetle that survives in the parched Namib Desert in Africa by drinking the dew that condenses on its own body (see p.4). There are beetles that live in water and beetles that spend their lives entirely underground. Some are barely visible to the eye, while others, such as the goliath beetle, are the largest of all insects.

Beetles vary in appearance but their wings are their most characteristic feature. A beetle has two pairs of wings. The front wings are thick and hard and act as covers for the more delicate back wings when the latter are folded away. In fact, the scientific name of the beetle group is Coleoptera, which means shield wings.

Beetle life cycle

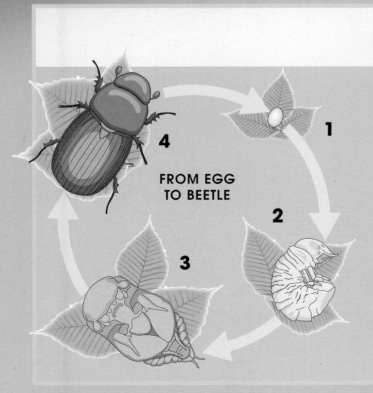

FROM EGG TO BEETLE

In developing from egg to adult, beetles undergo a complete metamorphosis. The details of development vary between groups, but the basic process is similar for all beetles.

1 Eggs are laid in the ground, in wood or in plants.
2 The egg hatches out into a wingless, wormlike larva, sometimes called a grub. This larva feeds and grows. As it grows, it molts several times.
3 When the larva is full grown, it stops feeding and enters the pupal stage, during which it is wrapped in a cocoon.
4 When the transformation is complete, it emerges as a winged adult.

Tiger, ground, and water beetles

Beetles have strong, chewing mouthparts and feed on almost every type of food. Some, such as tiger beetles, hunt ants and other insects. Like their namesakes, they move fast in pursuit of their prey. Water-living beetles, such as diving beetles and whirligigs, are also predators. Ground beetles are one of the largest families in the beetle group. There are more than 30,000 species living all over the world in every kind of habitat. Most ground beetles hunt other insects, but some species feed on plant matter.

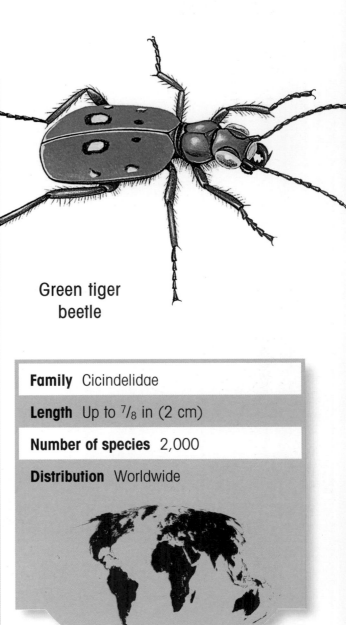

Green tiger beetle

Family	Cicindelidae
Length	Up to 7/8 in (2 cm)
Number of species	2,000
Distribution	Worldwide

Whirligig beetles

Whirligig beetles are amazing shiny black insects that can fly, swim, and move on the water surface. They get their name from their habit of spinning and whirling on the water. These beetles prey on other insects that fall into the water. Their eyes are divided into two parts so that they can see above and below the water surface at the same time. Whirligig larvae have feathery gills that enable them to breathe as they lie at the bottom of a pond or stream. They leave the water when they are ready to pupate.

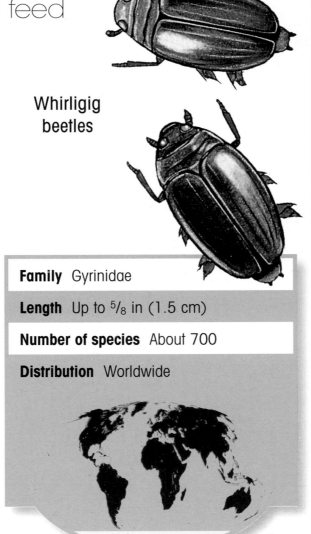

Whirligig beetles

Family	Gyrinidae
Length	Up to 5/8 in (1.5 cm)
Number of species	About 700
Distribution	Worldwide

Tiger beetles

Long-legged tiger beetles are fast-running hunters that catch smaller insects in their strong jaws. The larvae are also hunters; they live in burrows dug in the ground where they hide, waiting to grab passing prey. Although tiger beetles are found worldwide, they are more common in tropical and subtropical areas. Many are brightly colored and have a shiny, metallic sheen.

Diving beetles

Family	Dytiscidae
Length	Up to 1 1/2 in (3.5 cm)
Number of species	Over 4,000
Distribution	Worldwide

Diving beetle

Diving beetle larva

Diving beetles live in ponds and lakes. They swim by moving their long, fringed back legs like oars. When they dive, these beetles can stay underwater for some time, breathing air trapped under their wing cases. They are fierce hunters and can catch prey, including fish, larger than themselves. The larvae, known as water tigers, are predators too.

Bombardier beetle

Bombardier beetle

Family	Carabidae
Latin name	*Brachinus fumans*
Length	Up to 5/8 in (1.5 cm)
Distribution	North America

This beetle has an impressive way of defending itself. If attacked, it sprays boiling-hot chemicals out of the tip of its abdomen with an explosive pop. The spray is at a temperature of 212°F (100°C) and gives any predator a very nasty shock indeed. There are similar species living all over the world.

Caterpillar hunter

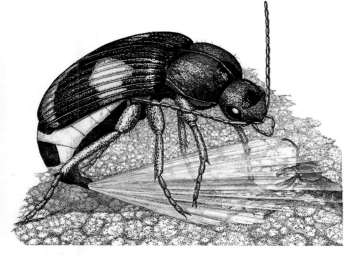

Caterpillar hunter

This large, shiny beetle is a member of the ground beetle family (Carabidae). As its name suggests, its main prey are caterpillars, and both adults and larvae even climb trees in pursuit of their victims. If attacked, the beetle gives off a foul-smelling liquid that can blister human skin. Ground beetles live in gardens, fields, and woodland.

Family	Carabidae
Latin name	*Calosoma scrutator*
Length	7/8– 1 1/4 in (2–3 cm)
Distribution	North America

Scarabs, dung beetles, and relatives

The scarab family is one of the largest beetle families and also contains some of the biggest beetles. Many are very colorful and they have unusual clubbed antennae, which can be spread out when needed for sensing odors. Some feed on plants, while others eat dung and other decaying matter. The burying beetle family feed on dead animals, performing a valuable waste-disposal service.

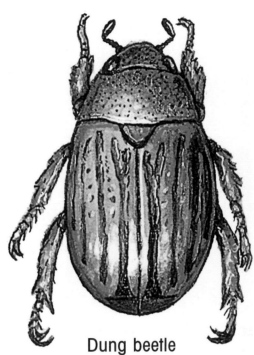

Dung beetle

Goliath beetles

African goliath beetles are some of the largest and heaviest of insects. They can weigh up to 3 ½ oz (100g). Females are smaller than males and are less brightly patterned. The male has a horn on the head, which is used in battles with rival males in the breeding season. Adult goliath beetles feed mainly on tree sap and fruit, climbing up into trees to feed.

Goliath beetle

Family	Scarabaeidae
Genus	*Goliathus*
Length	Up to 4 in (10 cm)
Distribution	Equatorial Africa

Dung beetles

This group of scarab beetles get their name from the habit of eating animal dung. The beetle rolls animal dung into a ball, buries itself with the ball, and then eats it. A beetle can eat more than its own weight of dung in a day. In the breeding season, the female lays her eggs in the center of a ball of dung. When the larvae hatch out they feed on the dung.

Subfamily	Scarabaeinae
Length	Up to 1¼ in (3 cm)
Number of species	5,000
Distribution	Worldwide, mainly tropical areas

Family	Silphidae
Length	Up to 1 1/4 in (3 cm)
Number of species	200
Distribution	Worldwide

Carrion beetle

Burying beetles

Burying beetles feed on carrion—animals that are already dead—so play an important part in recycling. Their flattened shape allows them to crawl under a small carcass, such as that of a bird or mouse. They then dig under the body so that it sinks into the ground. The female then lays her eggs on body. When the larvae first hatch they feed on a special liquid regurgitated by their parents, but later they feed on the decaying animal.

Rhinoceros beetle

This spectacular beetle is one of the largest of all insects. The male has huge pincerlike horns that make up about half his length. He uses these in battles with rival males over feeding sites or to win mates in the breeding season. One male can even pick up another with his horns and toss the rival to the ground. Although this beetle looks fierce, it is not a predator and feeds only on rotting plant matter. The female is smaller and has no horns. She lays her eggs in decaying wood, on which the larvae feed.

Family	Scarabaeidae
Latin name	Dynastes hercules
Length	Up to 7 in (18 cm)
Distribution	Central and South America

Rhinoceros beetle

Ten-lined june beetle

This beetle is usually active at night and is attracted to lights. It feeds on leaves and flowers, and sometimes causes damage to food crops. The female lays her eggs in the ground. When the larvae hatch they burrow into the ground, where they feed on plant roots. They also pupate underground.

Family	Scarabaeidae
Latin name	Polyphylla decimlineata
Length	1 1/3–1 1/2 in (2.5–3.5 cm)
Distribution	Western North America

Ten-lined june beetle

Rove beetles, ladybirds, and relatives

These families of beetles all contain large numbers of species and are widely distributed. Ladybugs are among the most familiar of all beetle families and are valued by gardeners and farmers because they feed on insect pests such as aphids.

Ladybug

Family	Coccinellidae
Length	Up to $^3/_8$ in (1 cm)
Number of species	5,000
Distribution	Worldwide

Rove beetles

This is one of the largest families of beetles and there are thought to be many more tropical species yet to be named. A typical rove beetle has a long body and short wing cases that cover only a little of the abdomen. When disturbed, it holds up the back end of its body, in the same way as a scorpion. Both adult rove beetles and their larvae prey on insects and other small creatures such as worms.

Family	Staphylinidae
Length	Up to $^7/_8$ in (2 cm)
Number of species	At least 45,000
Distribution	Worldwide

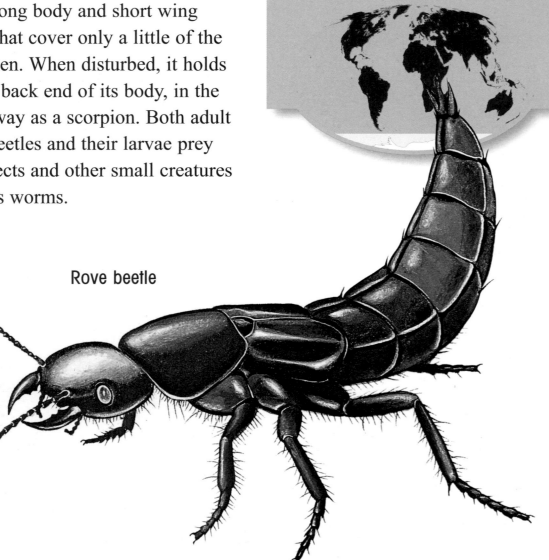

Rove beetle

Ladybug beetles

The ladybug's round, shiny, often spotted, body makes it one of the most easily identified of all insects. The color and number of spots vary among the many species, but a typical example has reddish orange wing covers and black spots. Adults and larvae feed mainly on aphids, which can be serious pests for farmers and gardeners. The ladybug's bright colors warn its enemies that it tastes unpleasant and may be poisonous. Ladybugs often hibernate under logs, bark, or piles of leaves, or in attics.

Fireflies

Fireflies, also known as glow-worms, are a type of beetle that can produce a yellowish green light in a special area at the end of the abdomen. Each species of firefly flashes its light in a particular pattern to attract mates of its own kind. Male fireflies have wings, but females are often wingless and look like larvae. Fireflies usually glow at dusk and can shut off their light when it's not required. In some species, adults do not feed, but others eat pollen and nectar.

Firefly

Family	Lampyridae
Length	Up to 1⅛ in (2.5 cm)
Number of species	2,000
Distribution	Worldwide in temperate and tropical regions

Blister beetle

Family	Meloidae
Length	Up to 1½ in (3.5 cm)
Number of species	2,500
Distribution	Worldwide

Red-blue checkered beetle

The brightly colored beetles in this family usually live on flowers, where they lie in wait for the tiny insects on which they feed. This species lays its eggs on flowers. When the larvae hatch, they hitch a ride with visiting bees and wasps, and are carried back to their nests where they prey on their larvae.

Family	Cleridae
Latin name	*Trichodes nutalli*
Length	⅜ in (1 cm)
Distribution	Eastern North America

Red-blue checkered beetle

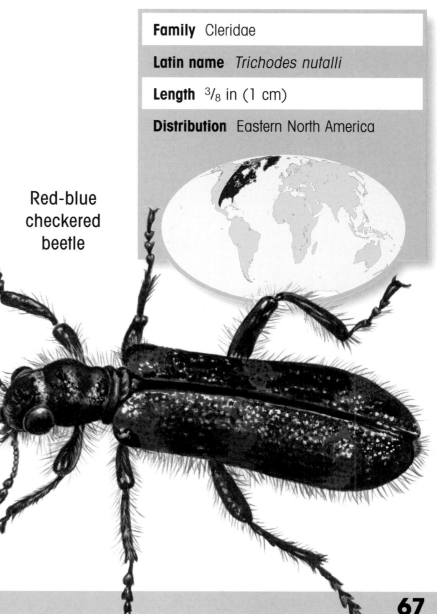

Blister beetles

Also known as oil beetles, these insects contain a substance called cantharidin. If the beetle is disturbed, the smelly oily liquid oozes from its body. It has been used as a treatment for skin warts. Blister beetles generally live on flowers. Some larvae feed on grasshopper eggs, others attach themselves to bees, and if carried back to the bees' nest, feed on the eggs, bee larvae, and pollen stores.

Insects that glow

A few types of beetle and other insects have developed an amazing ability to glow in the dark. Chemical reactions inside the body produce a natural light, called bioluminescence, which the insects use to attract mates, lure prey, or ward off attackers.

Right This glistening curtain may look pretty but, in fact, each thread is a trap made by the fungus gnat to catch prey.

Fungus gnat

Fungus gnats are tiny, flylike insects that live in caves and other dark damp places. They are best known for their glowing, wormlike larvae, which have developed an unusual method of catching prey. The nest of the fungus gnat larvae is a transparent tube of mucus. From the tube hangs a curtain of silk threads, each covered in droplets of glue. The larva lies in its tube, waving its glowing tail to light up the threads. Midges, moths, and other insects are attracted to the shining curtain and are trapped by its threads. The larva pulls in the threads and gobbles up its catch.

Above The light at the tip of the fungus gnat larva's tail is made chemically inside its body.

The railroad worm

This creature is not a worm at all but the female of a kind of beetle. It comes out at night to hunt for food. If threatened or in danger, it switches on the bright lights on its head and body to warn the attacker to stay away. The head glows a fiery red and the body a pale, greenish yellow. It also lights up when attacking other creatures, and it kills its prey with a poisonous bite. Railroad worms have even been known to eat others of their own species. The lights are produced by a chemical reaction inside the insect's body. By day it appears drab brown and hides away under logs or rocks.

Glowworms

The glowworm is also a kind of beetle. It makes a yellowish green light by a chemical reaction inside the body. Glowworms flash their lights in the darkness to attract mates. Each species has its own pattern of flashes. They use different lengths of flashes and can change the frequency and brightness of their signals. In some species, it is the male who flashes to attract the female, while in other species, the females make the first move. The female stops producing light after she has mated. Some glowworms use their lights to warn enemies that they taste nasty and should be left alone.

Left A Douglas fir glowworm shows off her glowing abdomen to attract any males that may be nearby.

Wood-eating beetles

The beetles of these beetle families all feed on wood at some stage of their lives. Some feed on dead and rotting trees and provide a valuable recycling service. The larvae of other beetles feed on live trees and on wood used in furniture and housing and cause serious damage.

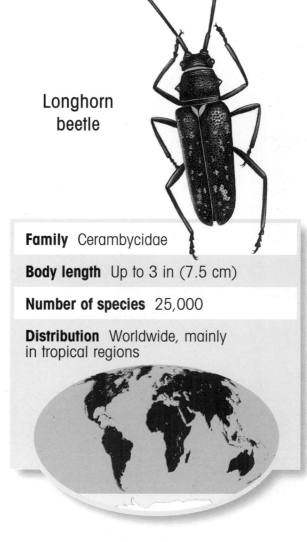

Longhorn beetle

Family	Lucanidae
Length	Up to 3 in (7.5 cm)
Number of species	900
Distribution	Worldwide

Family	Cerambycidae
Body length	Up to 3 in (7.5 cm)
Number of species	25,000
Distribution	Worldwide, mainly in tropical regions

Male stag beetles

Stag beetles

With their large heads and massive jaws, male stag beetles are among the most spectacular of all insects. The jaws of the male are branched like the antlers of a stag and, like stags, these beetles battle with one another to win females. The beetle with the largest jaws usually wins the contest. Despite their fearsome appearance, these insects feed mostly on tree sap and other liquids. Females lay their eggs in cracks in logs or dead tree stumps. The larvae feed on the juices of the rotting wood.

Longhorn beetles

Although these beetles occur all over the world, they are most common in tropical areas. They have extremely long antennae, which can be up to three times the length of the body. Adult longhorns feed on pollen and nectar. The female lays her eggs in the crevices of trees or logs. When the larvae hatch, they tunnel into the wood as they feed and may cause considerable damage. The larvae also eat plant roots.

Metallic wood-boring beetles

Also known as jewel beetles, these insects are often brightly colored. They live in woodland, usually in tropical areas, where the adults feed on flower nectar and leaves. The eggs are laid on trees and branches, and the larvae feed on the wood when they hatch.

Metallic wood-boring beetle

Family	Buprestidae
Length	Up to 3$\frac{1}{16}$ in (8 cm)
Number of species	25,000
Distribution	Mainly in tropical regions

Harlequin beetle

This large beetle gets its common name from its colorful markings. It generally lives on tree trunks in tropical rainforests and feeds on sap. The legs of the male are usually longer than his body and he can move fast. The female lays her eggs in small holes chewed in tree bark. When the larvae hatch they tunnel into the wood and feed on it. They pupate deep in the wood and emerge as adults.

Family	Cerambycidae
Latin name	Acrocinus longimanus
Length	Up to 3 in (7.5 cm)
Distribution	Central and South America

Harlequin beetle

Family	Anobiidae
Latin name	Xestobium rufovillosum
Length	$\frac{3}{8}$ in (1 cm)
Distribution	Europe, introduced in North America

Deathwatch beetle

Adult deathwatch beetles live on flowers, but the females lay their eggs in cracks in wooden furniture or buildings. When they hatch, the larvae tunnel into the wood as they feed. They pupate in the wood and when the adults emerge they leave telltale holes in the surface. The beetles make a clicking sound as they bang their heads against their wooden tunnels in order to attract mates. This was once thought to be a warning of death, hence the common name of this species.

Deathwatch beetle

Plant-eating beetles

All of these groups of beetle feed on plants. In some cases, the larvae eat the roots as well as leaves, damaging the plant. One family, known as weevils, is the largest of all beetle families and indeed of all families of living things. It contains more than 40,000 species found worldwide. Weevils are also known as snout beetles because of their long, beaklike snout. The leaf beetle family, Chrysomelidae, is second only to the weevils in the number of species it contains.

Family	Chrysomelidae
Latin name	*Leptinotarsa decimlineata*
Length	$1/4$–$3/8$ in (6–11 mm)
Distribution	North America, parts of Europe and Central Asia

Boll weevil

Family	Curculionidae
Latin name	*Anthonomus grandis*
Length	$1/4$ in (6 mm)
Distribution	North America

This little beetle causes huge damage to cotton crops. The adult insect uses its long snout to bore in the seedpods—called bolls—and eats these and the buds. The female also lays her eggs in the bolls. When they hatch, the larvae live in the boll and feed on the seeds and fiber, and destroying the plant. Like most weevils, this insect has a long beaklike snout and unusual elbowed antennae.

Boll weevil

Colorado beetle

This distinctive beetle has five black stripes on each wing cover, and is well known for its habit of feeding on the leaves of potato plants. Adults and larvae can devastate plants, quickly reducing them to a blackened mess. Each female beetle lays 400–600 eggs on the underside of leaves. When the larvae hatch, they start to feed on the leaves of the plant. When they are fully grown after a couple of weeks of feeding, they crawl to the ground and pupate in the soil.

Colorado beetle

Click beetles

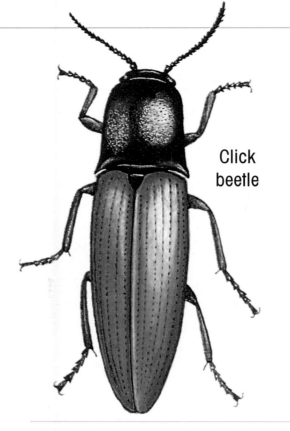

Click beetle

If touched or threatened, this large beetle folds itself up and falls to the ground. If it falls on its back, it rights itself with the help of a special mechanism on the body: a tiny spine on the thorax snaps into a groove on the abdomen and hurls the beetle upwards with a clicking sound. Click beetles may jump to a height of up to a foot (30 cm). Adults feed on leaves but their larvae, often called wireworms, eat seeds, roots, and other insects.

Family	Elateridae
Length	Up to 2 in (5 cm)
Number of species	7,000
Distribution	Worldwide

Leaf beetles

True to their name, these beetles feed on leaves and flowers. They lay their eggs on plants. Their larvae burrow underground and eat plant roots as well as feeding on leaves above ground. Some kinds of leaf beetles are serious plant pests. Many of the beetles in this family are brightly colored, often with a metallic sheen. They generally have short antennae.

Family	Chrysomelidae
Length	Up to ¹/₂ in (1.3 cm)
Number of species	35,000
Distribution	Worldwide (excluding polar regions)

Willow leaf beetle

Family	Attelabidae
Latin name	*Trachelophorus giraffa*
Length	1¹/₈ in (2.5 cm)
Distribution	Madagascar

Giraffe-necked weevil

Giraffe-necked weevil

The male of this extraordinary little weevil species has a very long neck that is up to three times the length of the female's. These weevils live in rainforests where they feed on the leaves of a particular type of tree, sometimes known as the giraffe-beetle tree. The female also lays her eggs on leaves and the male rolls the leaf up to protect the eggs and to provide food for the larvae when they hatch.

Above Wasps have strong jaws for biting into juicy fruit and for chewing up insect prey to feed to their young.

Wasps, bees, and ants

Wasps, bees, and ants belong to a large group of insects known as the Hymenoptera. They vary in appearance, but most have a definite "waist" at the front of the abdomen. They have chewing mouthparts and tongue-like structures for sucking liquids such as nectar from flowers. Not all members of this group have wings. Those that do have wings, have two pairs. The most primitive Hymenopterans are sawflies, which do not have the distinctive waist.

Right Worker bees busy in the hive. These are brood cells in which the queen bee lays her eggs and the young bees are reared.

Ant life cycle

Hymenopterans undergo a complete metamorphosis as they grow from egg to adult. They pass through a series of stages quite unlike the adult form. In a typical ant life cycle, most eggs hatch into wingless female workers, but a few hatch into queens or winged males.

FROM EGG TO ANT

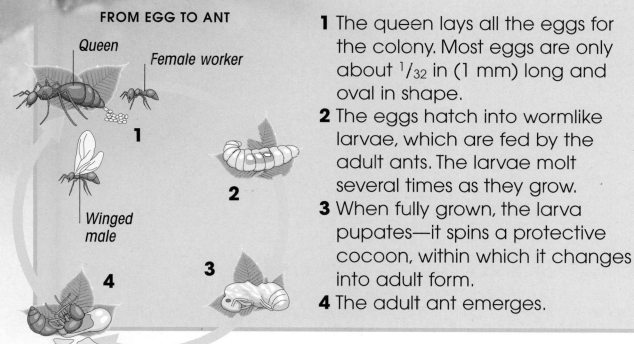

Queen

Female worker

1

Winged male

2

3

4

1 The queen lays all the eggs for the colony. Most eggs are only about $1/32$ in (1 mm) long and oval in shape.
2 The eggs hatch into wormlike larvae, which are fed by the adult ants. The larvae molt several times as they grow.
3 When fully grown, the larva pupates—it spins a protective cocoon, within which it changes into adult form.
4 The adult ant emerges.

Living together

Many hymenopterans live alone, but ants and some bees and wasps live in complex social colonies. Typically, a colony is headed by a queen, who is the only female to mate. Other females are workers, who build the nest, gather food, and care for young. These worker females do not generally lay eggs. There are far fewer males in a colony. They do not work and are usually present only at certain times of year in order to mate with new queens.

Bees 1

Although honeybees are well known for living in colonies, many kinds of bee live alone and make their own nests. These solitary bees, like their colony-living relatives, feed on nectar and gather pollen to feed their young. Their feeding habits make them important plant pollinators, just like honeybees.

Plasterer bee

Mining bee

Family	Colletidae
Length	Up to $1/2$ in (1.3 cm)
Number of species	3,000
Distribution	Worldwide

Mining bees

Mining bees nest in long, branching tunnels that they dig in the ground. Each bee digs its own nest, but large numbers may live close together. Each nest has a number of chambers and the bee stocks each one with some pollen and nectar. The female then lays an egg in each chamber and seals it off. When the larvae hatch they eat the food provided. Adult bees feed on nectar from flowers and are important pollinators. Most mining bees have short tongues.

Family	Andrenidae
Length	$3/8$–$7/8$ in (1–2 cm)
Number of species	About 3,000
Distribution	Worldwide, excluding Australia

Plasterer bees

Although plasterer bees live worldwide, they are particularly common in South America and Australia. They nest on the ground, digging tunnels that they line with a secretion from glands in the abdomen. This dries to a clear, waterproof substance. The female lays her eggs in separate chambers, provisioning each one with pollen and nectar for the larvae to eat when they hatch.

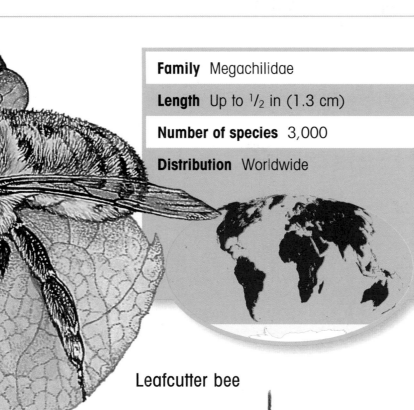

Leafcutter bees

Family	Megachilidae
Length	Up to ¹/₂ in (1.3 cm)
Number of species	3,000
Distribution	Worldwide

This type of bee is named for its habit of cutting circular pieces out of leaves with its jaws. It uses the leaves to line the chambers in its nest and then lays an egg in each one. Most leafcutter bees make their nest in this way, but a few species are parasites. They break into other leafcutters' nests and lay their eggs. When these larvae hatch they kill off the host's young and eat all the food. Adult leafcutters feed on nectar and collect pollen. They carry the pollen on hairs on the underside of the abdomen.

Leafcutter bee

Red mason bee

The red mason bee, like other mason bees such as the blue orchard mason bee of North America, is a solitary bee. These bees are very important plant pollinators and in fact pollinate more flowers, more efficiently than honeybees, so are becoming increasingly popular with gardeners. They nest in holes in places such as plant stems, bricks, and fence posts. Once the female has found a nest site, she stores some pollen inside, lays an egg, and seals it with a lid of mud.

Family	Apidae
Latin name	*Osmia rufa*
Length	³/₈ in (1 cm)
Distribution	Europe, North Africa, Middle East, Central Asia

Red mason bee

Cuckoo bee

Family	Anthophoridae
Latin name	*Nomada edwardsi*
Length	Up to ⁵/₈ in (1.5 cm)
Distribution	Western North America

This bee gets its name from its habit of laying eggs in other bees' nests. The female finds a host bee of another species in the process of stocking her nest with food. The cuckoo bee lays her egg inside the nest of the host bee. Later, the host bee lays her own egg, and seals the nest. The cuckoo bee larva hatches first and eats all the food in the nest.

Cuckoo bee

Bees 2

One of the largest bee families is the Apidae, which includes species that are extremely important pollinators, such as bumblebees and honeybees. Some members of the family live in colonies, but many are solitary. Bees eat nectar and feed their larvae on pollen, often mixed with nectar. Those that make honey use it as food for the winter or whenever it is hard to gather nectar.

Bumblebee

Bumblebees

There are about 250 species of bumblebee, mostly living in the northern hemisphere. They are large, hairy bees, usually black in color, with some yellow markings. Queens may be up to 1 in (2.5 cm) in length, workers are smaller. They live in small colonies. In spring, queens, which are the only bumblebees to live though the winter, look for underground nest sites. Each queen collects pollen and nectar and makes food called beebread. Later, she lays eggs and when the larvae hatch, they feed on the beebread. These larvae develop into adult worker bees and they take over the work of the colony while the queen continues to lay eggs.

Orchid bee

Family	Apidae
Genus	*Euglossa*
Length	Up to 1 in (2.5 cm)
Distribution	Central and South America

Orchid bees

There are about 175 different types of orchid bee of the genus *Euglossa*, some of which are brightly colored. All are strong fliers. Scientists have solved the puzzle of why male orchid bees visit orchid flowers, but do not gather nectar. The bees have little brushlike structures on their front legs, which they rub against the flower to pick up its fragrance. They then transfer this to special structures on their back legs. The scent attracts female bees to the male for mating. These bees are important pollinators of orchids—as they visit the orchids they pick up pollen and transfer it to the next flower.

Family	Apidae
Genus	*Bombus*
Length	Up to ³/₄ in (1.9 cm) (worker)
Distribution	North America, Europe, Asia

Stingless bee

Stingless bees

These bees cannot sting, but they do have biting jaws. Stingless bees live in large colonies and make nests under ground, in tree trunks, or even in part of a termite nest. They build up stores of honey as food for their young after hatching.

Family	Apidae
Genus	*Trigona*
Length	Up to ³/₈ in (1 cm)
Distribution	Tropical and subtropical Central and South America, Africa, Asia, Australia

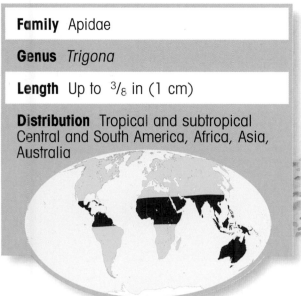

Stingless bee

Giant honeybee

These large bees live in colonies. They always make their nests above ground, hanging from a tree branch, or a cave or cliff ledge. Although these bees are very fierce and attack if their nest is disturbed, people do gather honey from the combs.

Family	Apidae
Latin name	*Apis dorsata*
Length	Up to ³/₄ in (1.9 cm) (worker)
Distribution	India, Southeast Asia

Carpenter bees

Carpenter bees get their name from the female's habit of chewing a tunnel-like nest in wood. She makes a row of separate cells inside the tunnel, fills them with pollen and nectar food stores, and lays one egg in each cell. She even stays nearby and guards the nest. The larvae eat the pollen and nectar provided. Adults feed on flower nectar.

Family	Apidae
Genus	*Xylocopa*
Length	Up to 1 in (2.5 cm)
Distribution	North America

Giant honeybee

Carpenter bee

Making honey

Honeybees are the best known of all bees. They pollinate countless food crops and produce millions of dollars' worth of honey and wax every year. Honeybees live in huge colonies of thousands of bees, with a complex social organization. Most of the members of the colony are female workers. They care for the young, build and repair the nest, and gather food, but they do not lay eggs.

Right In the summer months, honeybees make honey from flower nectar and store it in cells in the hive to feed on in winter.

Queen

Workers, drones, and queens

When a worker bee returns from a foraging trip laden with pollen and nectar, the others gather around to collect the food. Workers also make the nest cells, building them from wax produced in glands on the underside of their abdomen. The bees knead the wax with their mouthparts until it is soft enough to use for building. Male bees, also called drones, do not work and are produced only at certain times of year to mate with new queens. Each colony has a queen. The queen bee is larger than the other bees and lays all the eggs of the colony.

Drone   Worker

Bee dances

When a bee returns to the hive having found a good source of nectar and pollen, she performs a special "dance" to tell the other bees. If the food is close by she moves in small circles, first to the right and then to the left. The other bees soon fly off to find the flowers. If the source of food is further away, the bee dances in a figure of eight form with a straight run between the circles. The angle of the straight run corresponds to the angle of the food source to the sun. The quicker the dance is repeated, the nearer the food source.

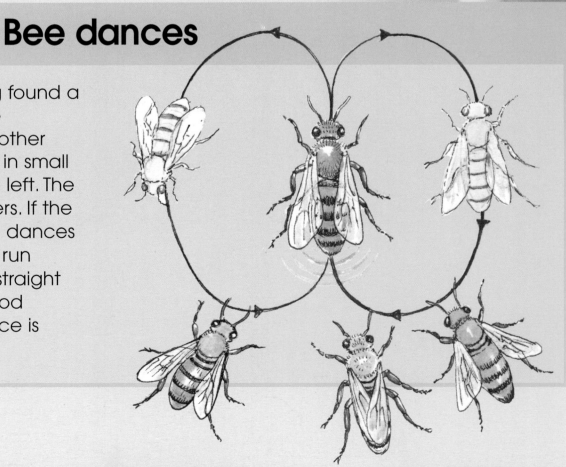

Worker bee's tools

Everything the worker bee needs is on its own body. On each front leg there are long hairs used to remove pollen from the body and a special notch for cleaning the antennae. On the middle legs there are fringes of hair for removing pollen from the forelegs, and a spike for taking wax from glands in the abdomen. On each hind leg there is a pollen basket—a special area lined with hairs where pollen is carried.

Hairs for removing pollen from body

Pollen basket

Sawflies, wood wasps, and horntails

These insects are the most primitive of the Thymenopteran group. Sawflies get their name from the sawlike egg-laying tube of the female; wood wasps have a similar tool. The larvae look like fat, hairless caterpillars but have more prolegs and only one pair of simple eyes. Adults look like wasps, but without the distinctive "waist" between abdomen and thorax. They are weak fliers and do not usually live long. Many sawflies are plant pests and some have been spread outside their native range in plant seedlings.

Common sawfly

Common sawflies

This is the largest family of sawflies. The female uses her egg-laying tube, or ovipositor, to cut slits in the stems and leaves of plants into which she lays her eggs. The larvae feed on leaves when they hatch. Many of these sawflies cause damage to trees and garden plants. One, for example, is a pest of larch trees and another, known as the currant-worm, damages currant and gooseberry bushes.

Family	Tenthredinidae
Length	$1/16$–$7/8$ in (0.2–2 cm)
Number of species	4,000
Distribution	Worldwide, excluding Antarctica

Stem sawflies

These are small, slender sawflies. The female lays her eggs on plant stems and the larvae bore into stems of plants, such as grasses and willows, to feed. When a larva is fully grown, it pupates on the ground, spinning itself a silk cocoon. Adult stem sawflies sip nectar from flowers. One member of this family, the wheat stem sawfly, has caused huge damage to wheat crops in western North America.

Family	Cephidae
Length	Up to $5/8$ in (1.5 cm)
Number of species	80
Distribution	Northern hemisphere

Stem sawfly

Conifer sawflies

The larvae of these sawflies feed on conifer trees and are serious pests in conifer forests, where they strip the needles from the trees. Males of this group of sawflies have broad comblike antennae. These are used for sensing pheromones—chemical substances released by females—when searching for a mate.

Family	Diprionidae
Length	Up to ½ in (1.3 cm)
Number of species	90
Distribution	Northern hemisphere

Conifer
sawfly

Horntails

These wasplike insects are named for the spine at the end of the abdomen, which looks rather like a wasp's sting. Female horntails also have a long ovipositor (egg-laying tube), which they use for drilling holes in rotting wood into which they lay their eggs. Horntail larvae also have a small spine at the end of the body. They usually live on conifer trees.

Horntail

Family	Siricidae
Length	⁷/₈–1¹/₂ in (2–4 cm)
Number of species	95
Distribution	Worldwide

Family	Orussidae
Length	Up to ⁵/₈ in (1.5 cm)
Number of species	75
Distribution	Worldwide

Parasitic wood wasps

This small family of sawflies have developed rather an unusual way of life and the larvae do not feed on plants. The female lays her eggs in the nests of other insects, such as wood-boring beetles and horntails. When the wood wasp larvae hatch, they kill and eat the host larvae. They are most common in Africa.

Parasitic wood
wasp

Wasps

Wasps may seem to humans to be irritating insects, but in fact they are very useful. Wasps feed their young on other insects, such as caterpillars and aphids, that can do serious harm to garden and food plants. Without wasps there would be many more of these pests. Adult wasps like to eat mainly nectar and other sweet things. They have strong jaws that enable them to bite into soft, ripe fruit. Some wasps live in colonies, but they do not store food and all members of the colony except the queen die in winter. She hibernates, living off her body fat. In spring she lays eggs and starts a new colony.

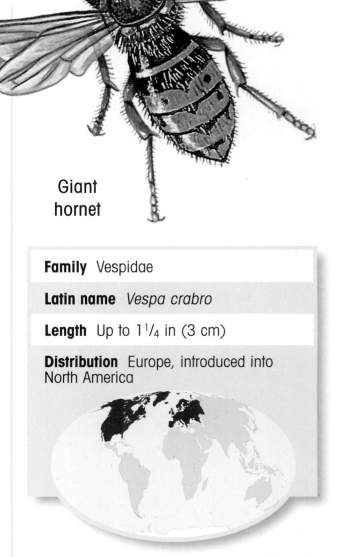

Giant hornet

Family	Vespidae
Latin name	*Vespa crabro*
Length	Up to 1¼ in (3 cm)
Distribution	Europe, introduced into North America

Sandhill hornet

These hornets make their papery nests close to the ground in shrubs and hedges in sandy country. They may also nest in roof eaves. If disturbed, they can give a severe sting. Adults eat nectar and larvae feed on insects that have been pre-chewed by adults.

Family	Vespidae
Latin name	*Vespula arenaria*
Length	⁷/₈ in (2 cm)
Distribution	Northern North America

Sandhill hornet

Giant hornet

This insect is a European species that was introduced into North America. Adult hornets feed on other insects. They live in colonies in nests built of a papery material that is made from chewed-up plants. The nest is usually in a hollow tree or an old building. The larvae eat insects caught by adults. Like other wasps, the hornet has a sting at the end of its body. This is a pointed tube, linked to a bag of venom. When the sting is pushed into the victim, venom flows through the tube. The hornet can pull out its sting and use it again.

Spider wasps

Spider wasp

Adults of this family of large wasps feed on nectar. The female caches spiders to feed to her young—hence the name. She paralyzes the spider with her sting, and then places it in a cell of her nest along with an egg and seals the top with mud. When the wasp larva hatches, it eats the spider.

Family	Pompilidae
Length	Up to 2 in (5 cm)
Number of species	4,000
Distribution	Worldwide

Yellow jackets

Yellow jackets, or common wasps, feed on nectar and other sweet things, such as ripe fruit. They also catch other insects to feed to their young. Wasps are well known for their sting. The pointed sting is at the end of the body and is linked to a bag of venom. The wasp uses its sting to attack prey and to defend itself against enemies—including humans. The wasp's bright colors probably act as a warning—keep away or else! When a creature such as a bird attacks a wasp and gets stung, it learns to link the black and yellow stripes with the painful sting. This makes it less likely that it will attack another wasp.

Family	Vespidae
Genus	*Vespula*
Length	Up to ⅝ in (1.5 cm)
Distribution	North America, Europe, Asia, North Africa, Australia, New Zealand

Yellow jacket

Mud daubers

Mud dauber

Mud wasps are solitary wasps that feed on other insects and nectar. The female makes a nest of damp mud. Into each cell she puts an egg and some insects that she has paralyzed with her sting for her young to eat when it hatches.

Family	Sphecidae
Length	⅜–1¼ in (1–3 cm)
Number of species	8,000
Distribution	Worldwide

Wasps' nests

Wasps are among the most skilled builders in the insect world. Some make their own nests in which they lay their eggs and which they stock with food for when the young hatch. Others gather in large colonies and build much more complex structures of mud or chewed wood pulp.

Paper wasps

The paper wasp starts its nest alone. A female makes a series of papery envelopes out of chewed up wood fiber, mixed with her own spit. The result looks rather like grayish brown paper. She then lays an egg in each chamber of the nest. Once her first batch of young mature, they become the workers and the founding female stops work to become the queen of the colony and devote herself to laying more eggs. The workers expand the nest and feed the young. In autumn most wasps in the colony die, leaving only one fertilized young queen, who hibernates through the winter, ready to start a new colony the following spring.

Above A paper wasp nest usually contains 20–30 adults and one queen. There is no outer covering and the egg cells are open to the air.

Left European hornets inside their nest, which is shaped like a teardrop and covered with a thin and papery outer shell.

Mud nests

Potter wasps, or mud daubers, live alone, not in colonies. The female builds a pot-shaped nest of mud and water on the ground or on a wall or branch. Inside there may be a number of cells. She places an egg in each cell as well as food such as caterpillars or other larvae, which she has stung and paralyzed. The chamber is then sealed. When the wasp larva hatches, it eats the food left for it, then breaks out of the chamber.

Parasol wasps

These wasps make an open, fan-shaped nest, which usually hangs from a branch. The nest has no covering and during the day the wasps cluster underneath to protect their young. They may fan their wings to keep the young cool. At night the wasps leave the nest to find food, which they bring back to the growing larvae.

Above A female potter wasp carries a caterpillar she has captured back to her mud nest to provide a food store for her young.

Parasitic wasps

These wasps are not true parasites because parasites, such as fleas and lice, do not usually kill their hosts—it is in their interests for the host to stay alive. The hosts of parasitic wasps always die, but by that time the wasps have no further use for them. Many of these wasps inject a venom into the host as they lay their eggs. This paralyzes the host, making it an easy victim.

Family	Mutillidae
Length	1/4–1 1/8 in (0.6–2.5 cm)
Number of species	5,000
Distribution	Worldwide

Giant ichneumons

The female ichneumon can use her ovipositor to bore through wood to lay her eggs near the larva of another insect. When the egg hatches, the ichneumon larva eats the host larva. This wasp usually lays its egg near horntail larvae. The female can detect the movements of the larvae in wood with her long antennae.

Family	Ichneumonidae
Genus	*Megarhyssa*
Length	Up to 3 in (7.5 cm)
Distribution	North America

Ovipositor

Giant ichneumon

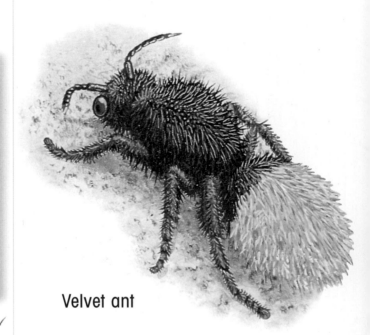

Velvet ant

Velvet ants

Velvet ants are not ants at all but wasps, with a thick covering of hair on their bodies. Male velvet ants have wings, but the females do not, making them look rather like ants. The females search for the nests of bees and other kinds of wasp. Having located a suitable host, they lay their eggs on the host's larvae. When the velvet ant larva hatches, it eats its host.

Brachonid wasps

Although there are 20,000 named species in this family, experts believe there are many thousands more yet to be discovered. The braconids vary widely in appearance, some being brightly colored and others dark and inconspicuous. Females lay their eggs on the larvae of other insects, often moth caterpillars. When the larvae hatch, they feed on the host's flesh. They emerge from the host caterpillar to pupate on its body, but the caterpillar usually dies before the adults come out of their cocoons. Adult braconids feed on nectar.

Brachonid wasp

Brachonid wasp eggs on host caterpillar

Family Braconidae

Length Up to 1¼ in (3 cm)

Number of species 20,000

Distribution Worldwide

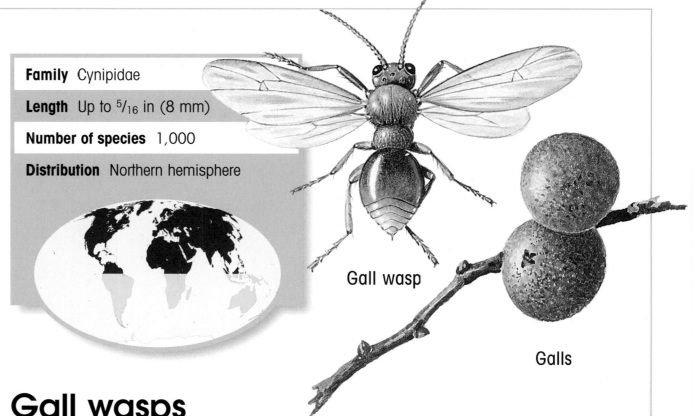

Family Cynipidae

Length Up to ⁵/₁₆ in (8 mm)

Number of species 1,000

Distribution Northern hemisphere

Gall wasp

Galls

Gall wasps

Most of these insects live in the northern hemisphere, although there are a few species in South America and South Africa. Gall wasps lay their eggs on a particular species of plant, which differs according to the species. The host plant forms a growth, called a gall, around the egg and when the larva hatches, it feeds on the gall tissue. Until relatively recently, oak galls were an important ingredient in the making of ink.

Chalcid wasps

Experts think there are many more species of these tiny wasps yet to be discovered. They are very common and are generally seen on flowers and leaves. Females lay their eggs on the larvae of other insects, such as moths, butterflies, and flies. When the larvae hatch, they feed on their host. One of the smallest of all insects— measuring only about one-tenth of a millimetre in length—is a member of this family.

Family Chalcidae

Length Up to ⁵/₁₆ in (8 mm)

Number of species 19,000

Distribution Worldwide

Chalcid wasp

Ants 1

Ants live in huge well-organized colonies comprising thousands of individuals. Most colonies construct a nest of interconnecting tunnels in rotting wood or under the ground. Each colony includes at least one queen ant, who lays the eggs. The worker ants are female, but cannot lay eggs. The worker ants gather food and look after eggs and young. The eggs are fertilized by fertile males, called drones. Worldwide there are at least 10,000 species of ants and experts think there may be as many as 5,000 more species yet to be discovered. All ants belong to a single enormous family, the Formicidae.

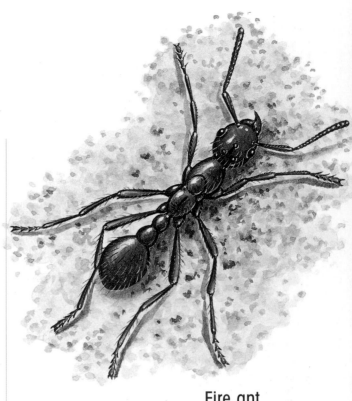

Fire ant

Family	Formicidae
Genus	*Solenopsis*
Length	1/4 in (6 mm) (workers)
Distribution	Worldwide

Red ants

Family	Formicidae
Genus	*Formica*
Length	Up to 1/2 in (1.3 cm) (workers)
Distribution	North America, Europe, Asia (temperate regions)

The main food of red ants is aphid honeydew, a sweet liquid that is a by-product of the digestive system of these tiny bugs. The ant strokes the aphid to encourage it to release the sugary liquid from its body. Red ants also feed on flower nectar.

Fire ants

As their name suggests, fire ants have a powerful bite and sting, which is extremely painful even to humans. They hunt other insects, which they sting to death, but they also eat seeds, fruit, and flowers. These ants make nests in the ground or under logs or stones. As in all ant colonies, a number of winged males and females are produced at certain times of year. They fly out from the colony and mate in the air. The males die and the females start new colonies.

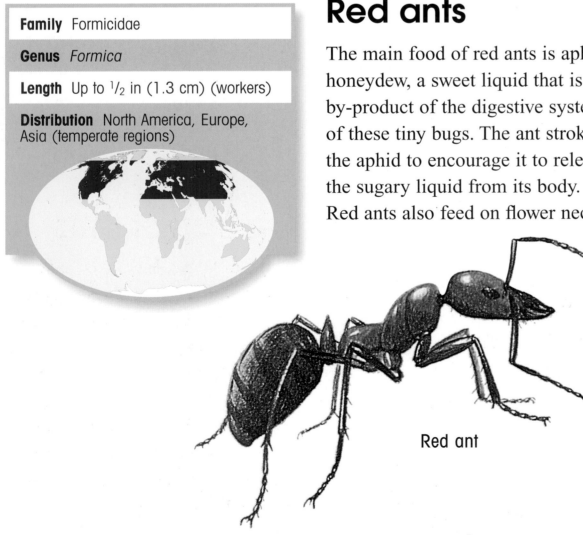

Red ant

Harvester ants

These ants get their name from their habit of feeding on seeds and grain crops. When the ants find a plentiful supply of seeds near their nest, they leave scent trails to lead others in their colony to the food. In times of plenty, the ants collect more seeds than they can eat and store them in special granary areas in the nest.

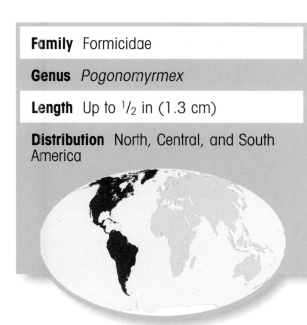

Family	Formicidae
Genus	*Pogonomyrmex*
Length	Up to ¹/₂ in (1.3 cm)
Distribution	North, Central, and South America

Harvester ant

Leafcutter ants

Most species of leafcutter ants live in tropical areas. Only one species, the Texas leafcutting ant, is found in North America. These ants grow their own food. The workers cut pieces of leaves and carry them back to their underground nest, where they are used to make compost heaps. The ants eat the special fungus that grows on the compost. Their leaf-cutting habits can cause damage to fruit trees, such as plum and peach, and to other plants.

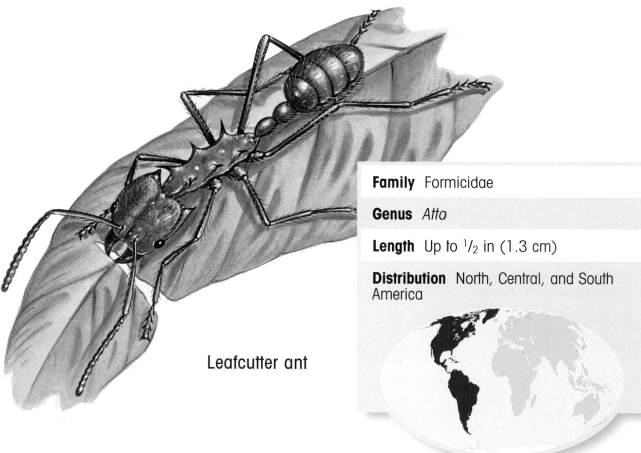

Leafcutter ant

Family	Formicidae
Genus	*Atta*
Length	Up to ¹/₂ in (1.3 cm)
Distribution	North, Central, and South America

Carpenter ants

Colonies of carpenter ants make their nests in wooden buildings or rotting tree trunks. They do not eat the wood, simply burrow into it, but can nevertheless cause structural damage. They feed on other insects, the juice of ripe and rotting fruit, and other sweet things. They also eat honeydew, a sweet liquid made by aphids and scale insects.

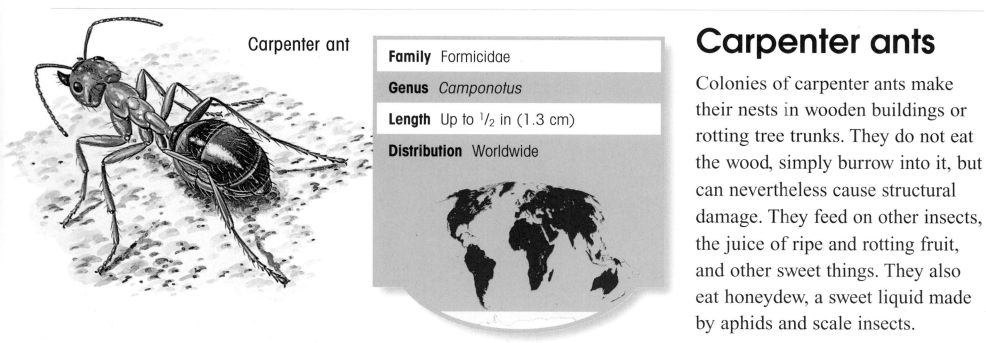

Carpenter ant

Family	Formicidae
Genus	*Camponotus*
Length	Up to ¹/₂ in (1.3 cm)
Distribution	Worldwide

Ants 2

No ant lives alone. Different species, however, make very different nests. Some make nests underground, others build nest mounds, and army ants manage without a permanent nest.

Mexican honeypot ant

These ants live in dry areas where food is sometimes scarce. They have evolved a system of storing food, using special members of the colony as living storage jars. These ants, called repletes, are fed with so much nectar and honeydew by the other workers that their abdomens become hugely swollen and they can no longer move around. They spend their lives clinging to the roof of the underground nest. In times of drought or food shortage, the colony can feed on these reserves. The ants simply stroke the repletes, thus stimulating them to regurgitate the food.

Bulldog ant

Bulldog ants

These are some of the largest of all ants and almost all the 89 species live in Australia. There is one species in New Caledonia. Fast-moving and aggressive, bulldog ants have a powerful sting and attack anything that disturbs their nest. They are thought to be one of the most primitive ant groups, and workers and queens are about the same size—usually queens are bigger than workers. They feed on small insects, seeds, fruit, nectar, and honeydew. Workers bring insects back to the nest to feed larvae.

Family	Formicidae
Latin name	*Myrmecocystus mexicanus*
Length	Up to $3/8$ in (1 cm)
Distribution	Mexico

Mexican honeypot ant

Family	Formicidae
Genus	*Myrmecia*
Length	Up to $1\frac{1}{2}$ in (4 cm)
Distribution	Australia

Army ant

There are about 200 different species of army ants. Most species live in tropical areas, including rainforests. Unlike other ants, army ants have no fixed nest. They are active during the day, traveling in huge swarms. At night they make temporary structures, known as bivouacs, usually in holes in the ground or beneath fallen trees. Sometimes the ants simply link their own bodies together to protect the queen and the larvae.

Family	Formicidae
Latin name	*Neivamyrmex opacithorax*
Length	Up to $^1/_2$ in (1.3 cm) (worker)
Distribution	Southwest U.S.A. to Costa Rica

Army ant

Southern wood ant

These ants live in colonies of thousands of individuals in nests, which may be several feet high. The nest is often started around a tree stump, which gives support. The ants use earth, twigs, leaves, pine needles—whatever they can find—to make a series of tiny chambers supported by columns and walls, and the mound takes shape. The system of tunnels and chambers for eggs and larvae extends well underground and up into the mound itself. Wood ants hunt other insects and bring prey back to the nest. They also keep aphids in the nest for the sweet honeydew liquid they produce.

Family	Formicidae
Latin name	*Formica rufa*
Length	About $^3/_8$ in (1 cm)
Distribution	Europe (including Britain), east to Russia

Southern wood ant

Weaver ant

Ants of this species make nests from leaves, which they fold and bind together with silk made by their larvae. A number of worker ants begin by pulling at the edges of a leaf. Once an ant succeeds at turning over an edge, the others join it and cooperate to fold the leaf. While some ants hold the leaf in position, the workers carrying larvae "sew" up the edges with silk from the larvae. The ants pass the larvae back and forth like spools of thread until the leaf is held together. Weaver ants are fierce hunters and eat any other insects they find. They also feed on nectar.

Family	Formicidae
Latin name	*Oecophylla smaragdina*
Length	$^3/_{16}$–$^3/_8$ in (0.5–1 cm)
Distribution	Tropical parts of India, Southeast Asia, Australia

Weaver ant

Above Lacewing larvae are fierce hunters. This green lacewing larva has just caught an aphid in its strong, pincerlike jaws.

Lacewings and relatives

The insects in this chapter are in three closely related orders. The largest group, the Neuroptera, includes around 6,000 species, such as lacewings, antlions, mantisflies, and owlflies. Although many of their names include the word "fly," none of these insects are true flies. Best known are the green lacewings, which are common in many gardens.

Metamorphosis

The other two orders in this chapter are very small. The Megaloptera includes insects such as dobsonflies and alderflies, and contains only about 300 species. The Raphidioptera, or snakeflies, has only about 200 species. All these insects undergo complete metamorphosis. They spend a much greater part of their lives as larvae than as adults, and the larvae hunt other creatures to eat. In fact, some such as brown lacewings are important pest controllers as they eat aphids. Neuropteran larvae generally have long tubelike mouthparts, used to punch holes in prey and suck out the body contents.

Left Owlflies spend much of the day resting, but at dusk, like their bird namesake, they fly off to hunt other insects.

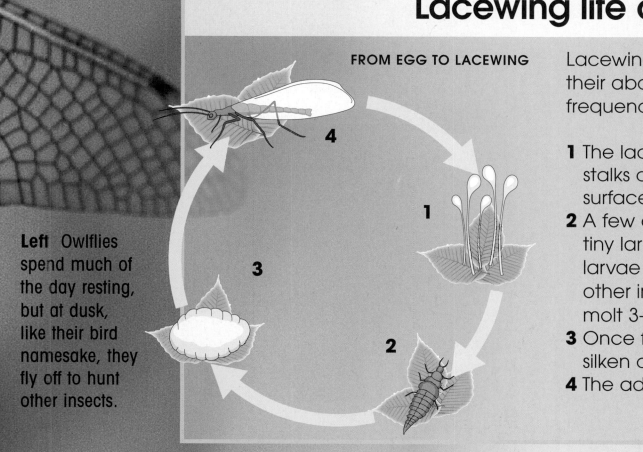

Lacewing life cycle

FROM EGG TO LACEWING

Lacewings attract mates by vibrating their abdomens to make very low-frequency songs.

1 The lacewing's eggs are laid on thin stalks and attached to leaves or other surfaces—even windows or walls.
2 A few days later the eggs hatch into tiny larvae. Despite their small size, the larvae are fierce hunters and feed on other insects or their eggs. They may molt 3–5 times as they grow to full size.
3 Once full grown, the larva spins a silken cocoon in which it pupates.
4 The adult emerges from the cocoon.

Dobsonflies, snakeflies, and alderflies

These insects are generally thought to have been some of the first to develop complete metamorphosis—a life cycle in which the larvae have a different form from the adult insects. The earliest fossils of these insects date from about 250 million years ago. Many of these insects spend most of their lives as larvae.

Square-headed snakefly

Snakefly

Family Inocelliidae

Length Up to ¹/₂ in (1.3 cm)

Number of species 21

Distribution Western North America, Europe

Snakeflies

The snakefly is named for its long snakelike neck, which it lifts as it searches for prey. Both adults and larvae hunt insects such as aphids and caterpillars. These insects are rarely seen as they tend to live high in trees and larvae often hide under bark. Adults have strong legs and are fast runners. They are active in the daytime.

Family Raphidiidae

Length Up to ⁷/₈ in (2 cm)

Number of species 185

Distribution Western North America, Europe, North Africa, Asia

Square-headed snakeflies

Some of the snakeflies in this family live in high-altitude pine forests, where the larvae feed on other insects and spiders living under the tree bark. The adults have two pairs of transparent wings with a dense network of veins, but they are slow clumsy fliers.

Alderflies

These dark-colored insects usually live near water. The larvae live in water for two to three years, often under stones, and feed on small insects. When fully grown, they leave the water to pupate on land. Adults live for only a few days—just enough time to mate and lay eggs.

Alderfly

Family	Sialidae
Length	Up to 1 in (2.5 cm)
Number of species	About 66
Distribution	North America, Europe, North Africa, northern Asia

Fishflies

The Corydalidae family is divided into two groups, the dobsonflies and the smaller fishflies. These insects are usually grayish in color and have long comblike antennae. They usually live and lay their eggs near water. When the larvae hatch, they crawl into the water where they remain, feeding on other insects until they are full-grown. They crawl out of the water to pupate. Adults are slow fliers and have short lives. They do not usually feed.

Family	Corydalidae
Genus	Corydalus
Length	Up to 2 in (5 cm)
Distribution	North, Central, and South America

Dobsonfly

Family	Corydalidae
Genus	Chauliodes
Length	Up to 1 in (2.5 cm)
Distribution	North America

Fishfly

Dobsonflies

Male dobsonflies have very large jaws, but these are mainly used for grasping the females during mating, not for feeding. Both male and female have large wings and flutter around at night. They lay their eggs near water and the larvae live on the river- or lakebed preying on other insects. Anglers often use the larvae, sometimes known as hellgrammites, as bait. The larvae leave the water to pupate, generally remaining in their cocoons through the winter. The adults emerge in spring and live only for a few days, long enough to mate and lay eggs.

Lacewings and antlions

L acewings, antlions, owlflies, and mantidflies all belong to a group called nerve-winged insects, or Neuroptera. They have two pairs of delicate, veined wings that can be folded like an arch over the body. Their larvae generally live on land and feed on other small creatures, which they catch in their powerful jaws.

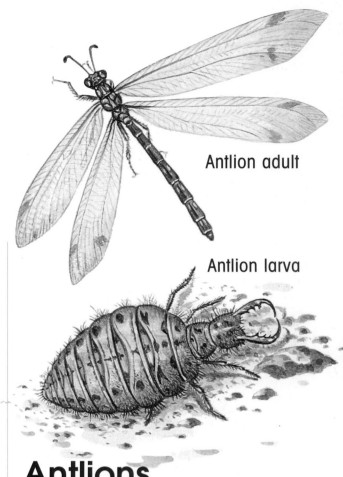

Antlion adult

Antlion larva

Green lacewings

These delicate insects have two pairs of pale green wings and large golden eyes. They are generally active at night, and feed on small insects, such as aphids, as well as pollen and honeydew. The larvae are fierce predators and many are used to control insect pests, including aphids. The larvae of some species carry bits of plants and the remains of their prey on their backs to keep them hidden so they can creep up on their victims.

Family	Chrysopidae
Length	Up to $7/8$ in (2 cm)
Number of species	1,200
Distribution	Worldwide

Antlions

Antlions generally live in dry scrub or sandy areas. They are best known for the hunting habits of the larvae of a few species. In these species, the larva digs a pit in sandy soil to trap passing insects. However, many kinds of antlions do not feed on ants and do not dig pits. They simply hide under stones and lie in wait for prey. Adult antlions look rather like dragonflies, but have clubbed antennae. They usually fly at night and probably catch other insects to eat.

Family	Myrmeleontidae
Length	Up to $1 3/4$ in (4.5 cm)
Number of species	2,100
Distribution	Worldwide, most common tropical and subtropical regions

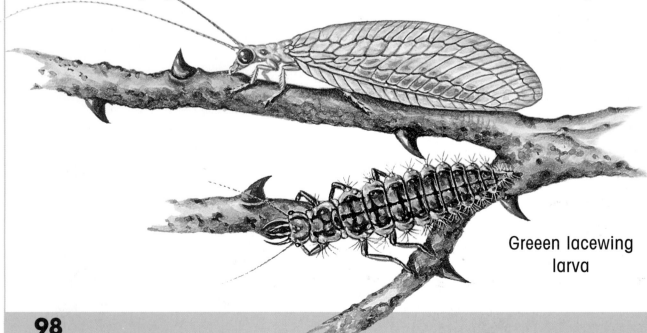

Green lacewing adult

Greeen lacewing larva

Mantidflies

Family	Mantispidae
Length	Up to 1 in (2.5 cm)
Number of species	400
Distribution	Worldwide, mainly in tropics

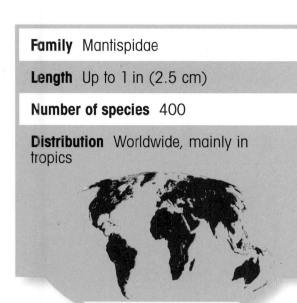

This relative of the lacewings looks like a small praying mantis and catches prey in the same way with its extra-large front legs. The larvae are also predators and some burrow into the nests of wasps and eat their larvae. Others feed on spider eggs.

Mantidfly

Brown lacewings

The insects in this family are smaller than the green lacewings and much less conspicuous. Most adults feed on other insects such as aphids, but some eat honeydew. They lay their eggs on plants. Brown lacewing larvae hunt aphids and other small insects, and can therefore be valuable controllers of insect pests on farmland.

Family	Hemerobiidae
Length	5/8 in (1.5 cm)
Number of species	550
Distribution	Worldwide

Brown lacewing

Owlflies

Family	Ascalaphidae
Length	Up to 2 in (5 cm)
Number of species	400
Distribution	Worldwide, temperate and tropical regions

These large insects look rather like dragonflies, but they have large clubbed antennae. They also have big, bulging eyes. When at rest, owlflies may cling to a twig with wings folded and abdomen sticking out at an angle. Like the birds after which they are named, they are usually active at dusk, when they catch flying insects such as caddisflies on the wing. The larvae live on the ground or in trees and lie in wait for prey. Ground-living larvae often camouflage themselves with bits of sand to conceal them from prey.

Owlfly

Attack and defense

As with larger animals, life in the insect world is a constant battle between predators and prey. Insects are hunted and eaten by many birds and mammals as well as by other insects, and they must find ways of protecting themselves from their enemies. And insects can be hunters, too. Some rely on speed to catch their victims. Others use traps and tricks that allow them to surprise their victims.

Below This saddleback caterpillar's showy coloration provides a warning that it is very poisonous. The hairs and spines are connected to poison glands.

Staying safe

Insects have many different ways of defending themselves. Some, such as many kinds of caterpillars, are poisonous and equipped with bristles and spines to deter predators. Often they are brightly colored to warn any potential enemy to stay well clear. Others rely on staying out of sight by looking like twigs or leaves (see pp.54–55). There are also insects, such as many butterflies and some bugs, including the peanut bug, that have a way of making themselves look bigger than they really are. These insects have large markings that look like eyes on their wings. The eyespots give a passing bird or other hunter the impression of a much larger creature that would be difficult to catch.

Left At rest, this owl butterfly reveals large eye spots on its back wings. These may serve to put off potential predators.

Antlion trap

The larva of the antlion is a fierce predator with spiny jaws. It sets a trap for its prey by digging a conical pit in sandy soil and sitting half-buried at the bottom. The pit has unstable sides, so that when a passing insect steps near the edge, sliding sand drags it down to the bottom—and into the antlion's waiting jaws.

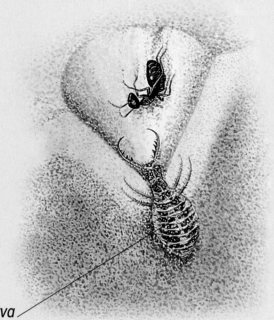

Antlion larva

Strength in numbers

Hunting in groups is a tactic employed by many different kinds of animals—notably ants. Working together, the ants can capture and overcome prey much larger than themselves. Raiding parties march out from the main colony in search of food. They swarm all over any victim, such as a larger insect or a millipede, and kill it with their bites. If the prey is small enough they carry it back whole for the rest of the colony, but larger catches are divided into pieces first.

Above A swarm of army ants cooperates in attacking a scorpion— a large and dangerous prey for such small predators.

Above The large eyes of a fly, such as this greenbottle, are made up of thousands of tiny hexagonal units, each with its own lens.

Flies, scorpionflies, and fleas

Flies are one of the largest insect groups; there are more than 124,000 known species. One of the few land-based creatures to survive in the Antarctic is a midge, a type of fly. Flies, after bees and wasps, are the second most important pollinators of plants and, by scavenging, they help to get rid of decaying waste. This chapter also includes scorpionflies and fleas.

Right A male dance fly presents a female with a gift of a froghopper bug before mating.

Mosquito life cycle

Most mosquitoes lay their eggs in water, where they float on the surface, or on aquatic plants.

1 A female mosquito lays single eggs or a group of eggs called a raft (pictured).
2 Each egg hatches into a larva, which lives in water and feeds on tiny food particles.
3 When the larva is fully grown, they pupate.
4 After a few days, the adult mosquito emerges.

FROM EGG TO
ADULT

One pair of wings

An important feature of flies is that they have only one pair of wings or none. In some species, the hind wings are reduced to small, knobbed structures called halteres, which help the fly to balance as it flies. A fly's wings beat fast and it is very agile in the air, hovering and even flying backward as well as forward. Some flies have extraordinary mating habits. The dance flies, for example, are fierce predators and the female is liable to eat any males that come near her. In order to divert her attention, the male dance fly catches an insect and wraps it up in silk. While hovering close to the female, he offers her this package. While she unwraps her gift the male takes the chance to mate.

Fleas and scorpionflies

Fleas are tiny wingless insects that live as parasites. They pierce the skin of birds and mammals, and feed on their blood. Some stay on their host all the time. Others live in the host's home or nest and leap up onto the animal to feed. Fleas can survive long periods without food, waiting patiently for the host's return. Scorpionflies are not true flies but a separate group of long-winged insects. There are about 550 species. Both fleas and scorpionflies undergo complete metamorphosis.

Hanging scorpionfly

Family	Bittacidae
Length	Up to $^{15}/_{16}$ in (2.2 cm)
Number of species	About 170
Distribution	Worldwide

Common scorpionflies

These insects get their name from the curving end of the male's body, which looks like a scorpion's sting. It is, in fact, the male's genitalia. Scorpionflies usually live in woodland and forests, where they feed mainly on dead insects, sometimes even daring to disentangle trapped prey from a spider's web. Their larvae also feed on dead insects.

Family	Panorpidae
Length	Up to $^{7}/_{8}$ in (2 cm)
Number of species	350
Distribution	North America, Europe, Asia

Common scorpionfly

Hanging scorpionflies

These insects have an unusual way of catching their food; adult hanging scorpionflies hang from leaves and twigs by their front legs and grasp passing flying insects with their back legs. Courting males often offer a dead insect to females before mating. After mating, the female usually lays eggs on the ground. When they hatch, larvae hunt on the ground and scavenge dead insects.

Cat flea

This flea can jump up to 200 times its own length, using its powerful hind legs, enabling it to leap up on to its hosts. The spiny combs on the flea's head help to anchor it in the host's fur, and it also holds onto the host's skin with its claws. The flea uses its piercing and sucking mouthparts to feed on the host's blood. Females lay their eggs in the nest or bedding of the host and the larvae feed on debris, including flea excrement. Cat fleas can also live on dogs and will bite humans.

Family	Pulicidae
Latin name	*Ctenocephalides felis*
Length	$1/16$ in (2 mm)
Distribution	Worldwide

Cat flea

Chigoe flea

Like other fleas, chigoes feed on blood. After mating, the female burrows into the skin of a human or other mammal, often between the toes or even under toenails. The area swells up around the insect leaving just a small hole for her to breathe. She feeds on blood and grows as her eggs develop. A week or so later she releases her eggs through the hole.

Family	Tungidae
Latin name	*Tunga penetrans*
Length	$1/32$ in (1 mm)
Distribution	Central and South America, Africa, and India (tropical regions)

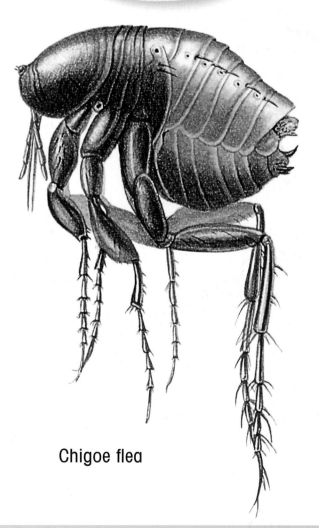

Chigoe flea

Oriental rat flea

Oriental rat flea

This common flea lives on the blood of rodents as well as other mammals, including humans. It can spread disease if it bites a human after biting an infected rat; this flea carried the Black Death, which killed millions in the 14th century.

Family	Pulicidae
Latin name	*Xenopsylla cheopis*
Length	$1/8$ in (3 mm)
Distribution	Worldwide

Long-horned flies

Crane fly

L ots of insects have the word "fly" in their name, but they are not true flies. The true flies are only those insects in the group Diptera. This group is generally subdivided into long-horned and short-horned flies. Long-horned flies are mostly long-legged, delicate flies with long antennae. Many, such as midges, occur in huge numbers and are an important food for other animals, notably freshwater fish. This group includes a number of bloodsucking insects, some of which carry disease.

Black flies

These small flies have stout bodies and humped backs. Males feed on nectar, but most females are bloodsuckers and give vicious bites as they feed from birds and mammals, including humans. Black flies often gather in huge swarms near water where they lay their eggs. The larvae attach themselves to stones or rocks with a suckerlike disk at the end of the body. They filter tiny particles of food from the water through fanlike structures on the head. In tropical areas, black flies may carry parasites that cause diseases such as river blindness.

Family	Simuliidae
Length	Up to $3/16$ in (5 mm)
Number of species	1,750
Distribution	Worldwide

Black fly

Crane flies

This is one of the largest of all the fly families. With their long, thin legs, crane flies look like large mosquitoes, but they do not bite or suck blood. Most adults live only a few days and probably do not eat. The larvae feed mainly on plant roots and rotting plants, although some are predators.

Family	Tipulidae
Length	Up to $2 5/8$ in (6.5 cm)
Number of species	15,000
Distribution	Worldwide

Midges

These tiny, delicate insects do not bite. They fly in huge swarms, usually in the evening, and are often seen near ponds and streams. They are particularly common in cooler regions in the far north and south of the world. Their larvae live in damp places or in water. Most feed on rotting plants and algae, but some are predators. A flightless midge of this family is one of the few creatures that lives on Antarctica.

Midge

Family	Chironomidae
Length	Up to $^3/_8$ in (1 cm)
Number of species	5,000

Distribution Worldwide (including Arctic and Antarctic)

Biting midges

Family	Ceratopogonidae
Length	Up to $^1/_8$ in (3 mm)
Number of species	5,500

Distribution Worldwide

Also known as punkies or no-see-ums, these tiny insects can give a painful bite. Some species bite humans to suck their blood. Others feed on the body fluids of other insects or eat the insects themselves. Larvae generally live in or around water, particularly still water, such as marshes and muddy pools.

Biting midge

Mosquitoes

Mosquito

Mosquitoes live all over the world. Although there are more species in warmer areas near the equator, the largest swarms are found in the far north during the brief Arctic summer. Mosquitoes are usually heard before they are seen. Their wings beat so fast—about 500 beats a second—that the insects make a constant whining sound as they fly. Males (and sometimes females) feed on nectar and plant sap. Most females also bite animals and suck their blood. They are most active at dusk and at night, but each species has its own time of activity.

Family	Culicidae
Length	Up to $^1/_4$ in (6 mm)
Number of species	3,000

Distribution Worldwide (including Arctic)

Feeding

Insects have an amazing range of diets. They feed on all parts of plants—leaves, roots, seeds, fruit, and even bark—and these plant eaters, such as grasshoppers, have strong jaws for chopping and chewing their food. Many insects are hunters; they catch other creatures to eat. Others, such as fleas and lice, live as parasites, feeding on the blood of other animals. And there are insects that feed on human food stores, such as grain, or eat their way through books, glue, and other household items.

Above A praying mantis feasting on a katydid it has captured. All mantids are predators and some even catch small creatures, such as lizards, as well as insects.

Above The female thread-waisted wasp hunts prey for her young to eat, not for herself. Caterpillars are the preferred food, so the wasp stings her victim to paralyze it and then takes it back to her nest. The wasp lays her eggs next to the caterpillar, which remains alive but cannot escape. When her young hatch, they have a meal available.

Liquid feeders

Many flies lap juices from rotting plant or animal matter, while others drink nectar and sap from plants. Some, such as black flies, suck blood from humans and other animals. But even flies that feed on solid food have to liquidize it first. They deposit saliva on the food, which partly dissolves it. They then mop up the resulting mushy liquid with the spongy pad at the tip of the mouthparts.

Above The feeding tube, or proboscis, of a moth or butterfly is coiled up under its head. When the insect needs to feed, it uncoils the tube, dips it into a flower, and sucks up the sugary nectar as if drinking through a straw.

Mosquitoes

Male, and sometimes female, mosquitoes feed on nectar and plant sap. But most females also bite and suck the blood of mammals—they need this protein-rich food so that they can produce eggs. In one meal the female can take twice her own weight in blood. To feed on blood, the mosquito pierces the host's skin with its special tubelike mouthparts. It then pumps some saliva into the wound to keep the blood flowing as it sucks. This saliva is what makes the bite itch.

Left A mosquito biting human skin. Certain mosquito species carry parasites in their bodies that cause an illness called malaria. These parasites enter the host's blood as the mosquito bites.

Short-horned flies

The short-horned flies are one of the two groups of true flies. This group includes species such as horse flies. They vary in size, but most have sturdy bodies and short antennae. The group comprises about 120 families and a wide range of life styles.

Horse flies

These flies have large, iridescent eyes. Males feed on pollen and nectar, but female horse flies feed on the blood of mammals, including humans. Instead of puncturing the skin, they make a small wound on the victim and then lap up the blood as it flows. Their bites can be painful and the flies can carry diseases. Females usually lay their eggs on plants overhanging water or damp ground. The larvae are fierce hunters, seizing other insects in their fanglike jaws.

Family	Tabanidae
Length	Up to 1 in (2.5 cm)
Number of species	3,000
Distribution	Worldwide

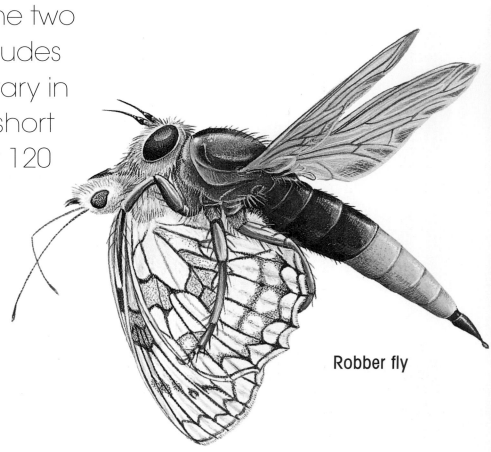

Robber fly

Robber flies

Fast-moving hunters, robber flies chase and catch other insects, including dragonflies, either in the air or on on the ground. They have large eyes for spotting potential victims and strong bristly legs for seizing their prey. Once a robber fly has caught its victim, it sucks out its body fluids with its short, sharp mouthparts. The larvae live in soil or rotting wood, where they feed on the larvae of other insects.

Family	Asilidae
Length	Up to 1¼ in (3 cm)
Number of species	5,500
Distribution	Worldwide

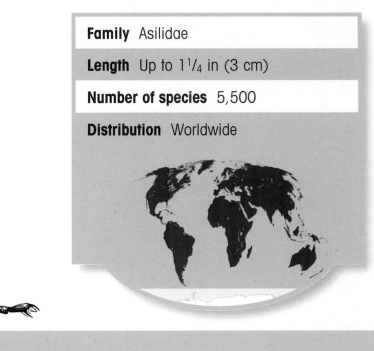

Horse fly

Bee flies

These stout, hairy flies resemble bees, hence their common name. Some also behave like bees as they hover in front of flowers feeding on nectar with the aid of their sucking mouthparts. The larvae are predators. The bee fly usually lays its eggs near the nest of another insect such as a bee or beetle. When the larvae hatch they enter the other insect's nest and feed on the larvae by sucking out their body contents.

Family	Bombyliidae
Length	Up to ⁵/₈ in (1.5 cm)
Number of species	5,000
Distribution	Worldwide

Bee fly

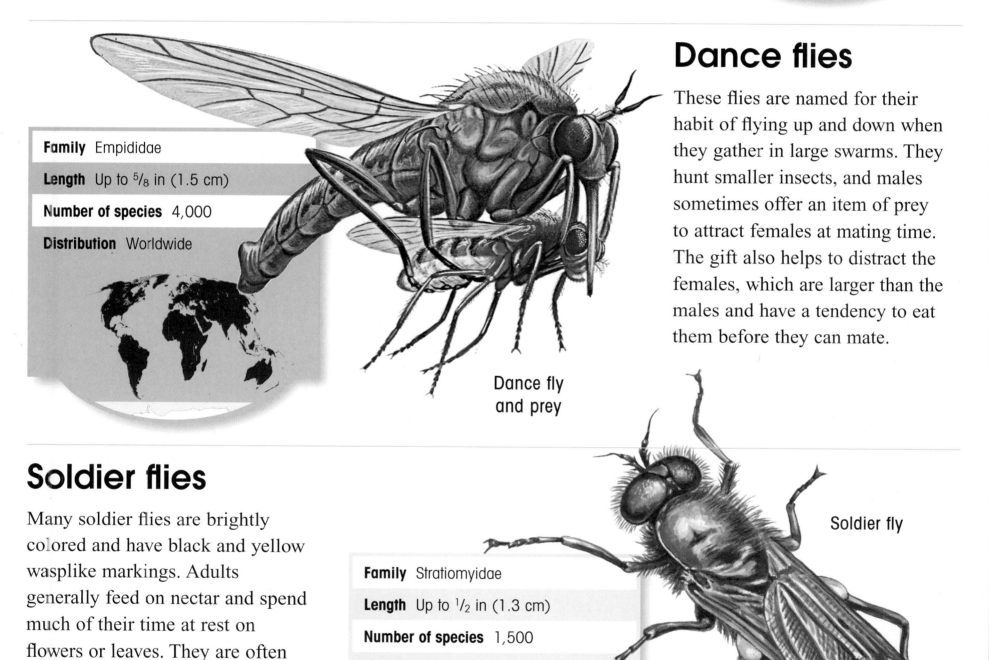

Dance flies

These flies are named for their habit of flying up and down when they gather in large swarms. They hunt smaller insects, and males sometimes offer an item of prey to attract females at mating time. The gift also helps to distract the females, which are larger than the males and have a tendency to eat them before they can mate.

Family	Empididae
Length	Up to ⁵/₈ in (1.5 cm)
Number of species	4,000
Distribution	Worldwide

Dance fly
and prey

Soldier flies

Many soldier flies are brightly colored and have black and yellow wasplike markings. Adults generally feed on nectar and spend much of their time at rest on flowers or leaves. They are often seen around compost heaps and other rotting matter. The eggs are laid near water, and the larvae live in water, feeding on algae and small creatures. They pupate in mud.

Family	Stratiomyidae
Length	Up to ¹/₂ in (1.3 cm)
Number of species	1,500
Distribution	Worldwide

Soldier fly

Flower flies, fruit flies, and relatives

These families, all short-horned flies, are generally thought to be slightly more advanced in their structure and development than the horse flies and relatives (see pp.110–11). One of these advances is the way the larvae transform into pupae. In other groups, the fully grown larva discards its final larval skin and then pupates. In these flies, the larva becomes a pupa inside the final larval skin.

Flower fly

Flower flies

Also known as hover flies, adult flower flies feed on pollen and nectar and are often seen near flowers. They are expert fliers and can hover with ease and even fly backward. Many species are brightly colored and look much like bees or wasps. They do not sting, however. Some hover fly larvae hunt insects, such as aphids, others feed on plants or live in the nests of bees or wasps, where they feed on their larvae. Flower flies are important pollinators.

Tephritid fruit flies

These small flies are common around flowers and overripe fruit. Their larvae feed on plant matter and some are serious pests, causing great damage to fruit trees and other crops. They are sometimes known as peacock flies because males wave their patterned wings up and down when courting. Females lay their eggs on plants, often in fruit such as apples. When the larvae hatch they burrow into the fruit as they feed. When full grown, the larvae tunnel out and pupate on the ground. This is one of two large families of fruit flies. The other is Drosophilidae, which contains 3,000 species.

Family	Tephritidae
Length	Up to $^{11}/_{32}$ in (9 mm)
Number of species	4,000
Distribution	Worldwide

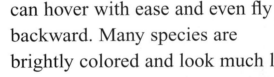

Family	Syrphidae
Length	$^{5}/_{32}$–1 in (0.4–2.5 cm)
Number of species	6,000
Distribution	Worldwide

Tephritid fruit fly

Stalk-eyed flies

Only two species of these flies live in North America and they have shorter eye stalks than others. As their name suggests, these flies have eyes that are on the end of long stalks either side of the head. Males generally have longer eye stalks than females, and females tend to mate with males with the longest eye stalks. In some species males engage in battles over females. Adults usually live in damp areas and feed on fungi and rotting plants. Larvae also feed on plant matter.

Stalk-eyed fly

Family	Diopsidae
Length	1/4 in (6 mm)
Number of species	150
Distribution	North America, tropical Africa and Asia

Thick-headed fly

With their slender stripy bodies, these flies look somewhat like wasps. They have a long structure called a proboscis on the head. Adult females are often seen around flowers, where they feed on nectar and wait for visiting bees or wasps. When a wasp or bee comes near, the thick-headed fly grabs it before it lands and lays an egg in its body. The larva hatches inside the host's body and feeds until it is ready to pupate, by which time the host has died.

Family	Conopidae
Length	Up to 1/2 in (1.3 cm)
Number of species	800
Distribution	Worldwide

Thick-headed fly

Toxomerus flower flies

These flies are beneficial to plants, and are therefore welcomed by gardeners. Adults feed on nectar and pollen and pollinate plants. Larvae feed on plant pests such as aphids.

Family	Syrphidae
Genus	*Toxomerus*
Length	Up to 1/2 in (1.3 cm)
Distribution	North America

Toxomerus flower fly

House flies, blow flies, and relatives

Also known as short-horned flies, a number of these insects feed and lay their eggs on rotting material such as dung and dead animals. This behavior may not sound very appealing, but in fact these insects are performing a valuable service in using and recycling this material.

Family	Calliphoridae
Length	Up to ⁵/₈ in (1.5 cm)
Number of species	1,000
Distribution	Worldwide

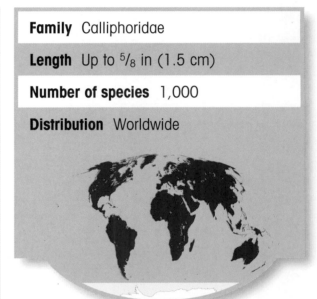

House fly

House flies probably came from central Asia originally, but have now spread all over the world and are very common wherever people live. They are extremely adaptable and feed on anything from garbage to animal feces. House flies have spongelike mouthparts and can only mop up liquid food. So when they land on a food item, they spit saliva onto the food to predigest it. They may also regurgitate partly digested food and mop it up again. House flies reproduce quickly, the female laying as many as 500 eggs in a few days. These hatch within a day and can grow to full size in less than a week. Adults emerge from pupae two to six days later.

Family	Muscidae
Latin name	*Musca domestica*
Length	Up to ⁷/₃₂ in (7 mm)
Distribution	Worldwide

House fly

Blow flies

These flies have stocky bodies with a metallic sheen. Adult blow flies feed on pollen and nectar as well as fluids from rotting matter. Many lay their eggs in carrion—the bodies of dead animals—or in dung, so the larvae have a ready food supply. Some blow flies even lay their eggs in wounds on live animals.

Blow fly

Dung fly

Many of the flies in this family feed on plants, but the dung fly preys on other insects, including flies. The female lays her eggs on cattle dung, while the male stays close by, guarding his patch of dung from other males. When the larvae hatch they feed on the dung.

Family	Anthomyiidae
Latin name	*Scatophaga stercoraria*
Length	Up to ³/₈ in (1 cm)
Distribution	North America

Dung fly

Bot flies

Family	Oestridae
Length	Up to ⁵/₈ in (1.5 cm)
Number of species	150
Distribution	Worldwide

Bot fly

Some kinds of these stout little flies can cause problems for animals, such as horses, sheep, and cattle. The adult flies lay their eggs on mammals and the larvae burrow into the host's skin to feed. A swelling, called a warble, develops around each larva. Eventually the larva leaves the host to pupate on the ground. Some bot flies live on humans, but lay their eggs on mosquitoes. The tiny larva holds on to the mosquito until it lands on a human to feed on blood. The bot fly larva then jumps off and burrows into the human's skin where it can cause a painful swelling. These flies are sometimes called warble flies.

Louse flies

Louse flies live as parasites on birds and mammals. There are two kinds: winged and wingless. The winged louse flies live on birds and have a flattened, dark brown body. Wingless species, often called keds, live on animals, such as sheep and deer, feeding on their blood. The female's eggs develop inside her body and she gives birth to live larvae, which also fed on blood. The sheep ked is a very common parasite and can stain the sheep's wool, reducing its value.

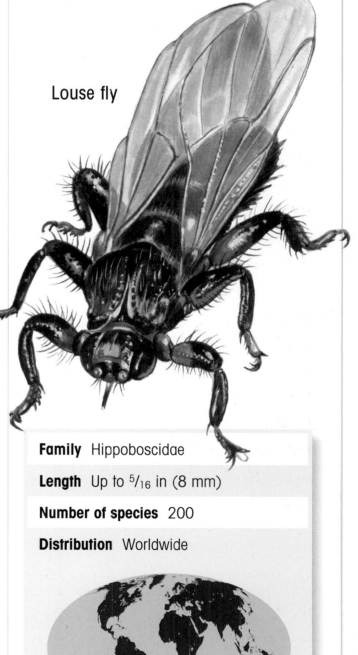

Louse fly

Family	Hippoboscidae
Length	Up to ⁵/₁₆ in (8 mm)
Number of species	200
Distribution	Worldwide

Life cycle

All butterflies and moths undergo complete metamorphosis from caterpillar to adult.

1 The eggs are usually laid on plants. A tiny caterpillar emerges from each egg after 1 to 3 weeks.

2 The caterpillar feeds greedily and grows so fast that it needs to molt several times.

3 When it is fully grown, the caterpillar stops feeding and enters the pupa, or chrysalis, stage. It finds a safe spot either in the soil or hanging from a little pad it spins from silk. Some moth caterpillars spin complete cocoons of silk around themselves.

4 Inside the pupal case, the caterpillar develops antennae, wings, and legs. Then the case splits and the adult emerges.

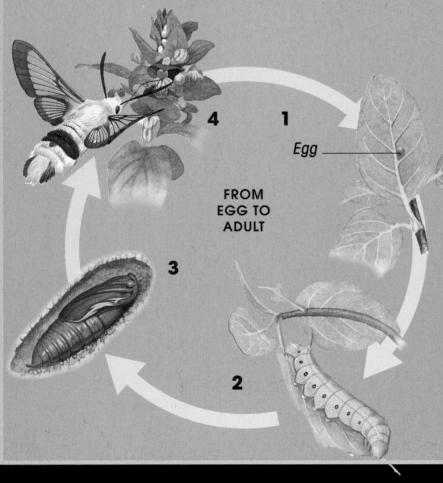

4   **1**

Egg

FROM EGG TO ADULT

3

2

Wherever plants grow there are butter
Known as the Lepidoptera, this is the s
group of insects, containing about 16
However, experts think that there may
Caddisflies look similar to butterflies a
in fact a separate group.

Butterfly or moth?

Butterflies and moths range from
a fraction of an inch long to the
of New Guinea, which have a w
(28 cm). Virtually all butterflies an
of wings that are covered with ti
All have antennae and sucking
food. Most butterflies are brightly
creatures, while moths are much
night, but there are many excep
butterfly or moth is called a cate
chewing mouthparts and spend
on plants and growing at an ast

Caddisflies and moths

Caddisflies look like moths, but they have hairs not scales on their wings. There are more than 40 families with about 11,000 species in all. Although moths are generally thought of as dull in color, many are brightly patterned. Like butterflies, moths have two pairs of wings covered in tiny scales.

Family	Geometridae
Wingspan	Up to 2⅝ in (6.5 cm)
Number of species	At least 21,000
Distribution	Worldwide

Large caddisflies

Caddisflies generally live near water. Adults survive only a few weeks and do not eat. Females lay their eggs in a mass of a jellylike substance on water plants. The eggs hatch into caterpillarlike larvae, which live in water and feed on algae. The larvae make cases around themselves from bits of leaf and twig held together with silk they spin from their own bodies. Some caddisflies live in cases fixed to the riverbed or another surface, and others can move around in their cases.

Family	Phryganeidae
Wingspan	Up to to 2 in (5 cm)
Number of species	79
Distribution	North America, Europe, North Africa, Asia

Large caddisfly

Measuringworm moth

Measuringworm moth caterpillar

Measuringworm moths

This is one of the biggest families in the butterfly and moth group. Most of these moths have slender bodies and fragile wings. When they are at rest during the day, they spread their wings out flat. Their caterpillars are known as inchworms or "loopers" because of the loop shape they make as they move. They eat leaves and are capable of causing serious damage to trees.

Clothes moth

The caterpillars of the clothes moth feed on hair and feathers in animal nests and on the dried corpses of small mammals and birds. Few creatures, other than some beetle larvae, can digest these difficult foods. Because humans use animal wool to make clothes, these caterpillars often come into our homes to feed on cloth. The adult moths are small and brownish in color, with narrow front wings that are folded neatly over the body when at rest. The adults do not usually feed.

Clothes moth caterpillar

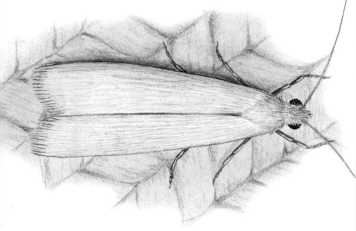

Clothes moth

Family	Tineidae
Latin name	*Tineola bisselliella*
Wingspan	$1/2$ in (1.3 cm)
Distribution	Worldwide

Tiger moths

Tiger moths have broad hairy bodies and boldly patterned wings. The bright markings of these moths and their hairy caterpillars warn birds and mammals that they are unpleasant to eat. The caterpillars, known as woolly bears, feed on plants that are poisonous to vertebrate animals and they store the poison for their own protection against predators.

Tiger moth

Family	Arctiidae
Wingspan	Up to $2^3/4$ in (7 cm)
Number of species	11,000
Distribution	Worldwide, more common in tropical areas

Atlas moth

This is one of the largest of all moths and is named for the maplike patterns on its wings. There are also some transparent scaleless patches on its wings, but no one knows the reason for these. The males have large feathery antennae that help them pick up the scent signals given off by females. Adults live for only a couple of weeks and do not feed. Caterpillars feed on plants such as guava and citrus fruits. When the caterpillars are ready to pupate they spin silken cocoons.

Atlas moth

Family	Saturniidae
Latin name	*Attacus atlas*
Wingspan	Up to 10 in (25 cm)
Distribution	Asia

Sphinx moths

Also called hawkmoths, sphinx moths are among the most powerful fliers of all butterflies and moths. Their wings beat so fast that they make a whirring noise and they can even hover like hummingbirds in front of flowers to feed. Like many moths, adults eat liquid food such as plant nectar. They suck up the food with a special tongue structure called a proboscis, which is hollow in the middle, and is kept rolled up under the head when not in use. Sphinx moths have the longest tongues of any moths and can feed on nectar at the bottom of tubelike flowers.

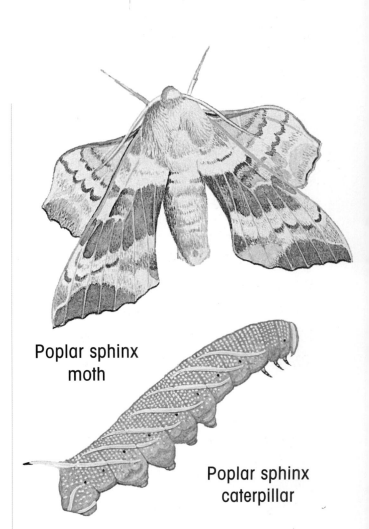

Poplar sphinx moth

Poplar sphinx caterpillar

Bee sphinx moth

Bee sphinx moth

One of a number of similar species, the bee sphinx moth plunges its long tongue deep into flowers as it feeds. With its broad, striped body and the large, clear areas without scales on its wings, this moth looks very like a bee as it hovers over plants. Unlike most moths, it flies by day, rather than at night. It lays its eggs on the underside of young leaves and the caterpillars are green or brown in color.

Family	Sphingidae
Latin name	*Sphinx hylas*
Wingspan	Up to 2³⁄₄ in (7 cm)
Distribution	Southern Asia

Poplar sphinx moth

The color and irregular shape of the poplar sphinx moth's wings help it hide on bark during the day. It lays its eggs on the undersides of leaves, often on poplar trees. Green with yellow markings, the caterpillars feed on the leaves of trees such as poplar and willow.

Family	Sphingidae
Latin name	*Laothoe populi*
Wingspan	Up to 4 in (10 cm)
Distribution	Europe, North Africa, northern Asia

Oleander sphinx moth

This is one of the most beautifully patterned of all moths. Adults rest on plants such as oleander during the day and then emerge at night to feed on nectar. The caterpillars are bright yellow at first but soon turn green with white and blue markings and large eyespots. These markings, which look like eyes, can fool a predator into thinking the caterpillar is a much larger creature than it really is. Oleander is the main food plant of the caterpillars. They pupate in yellow-brown cocoons on the ground.

Oleander sphinx moth

Family	Sphingidae
Latin name	*Daphnis nerii*
Wingspan	Up to 4 in (10 cm)
Distribution	Southern Europe, North Africa, Middle East to central Asia

White-lined sphinx moth

Adults of this moth feed on the nectar of flowers such as honeysuckle and clover. Like most moths, it has antennae that are extremely sensitive to smell. It can pick up the faintest scents, which helps it to find flowers at night. White-lined sphinx moth caterpillars are green with black stripes, and have a horn on the rear end.

White-lined sphinx moth

Family	Sphingidae
Latin name	*Hyles lineata*
Wingspan	Up to 3½ in (9 cm)
Distribution	Southern Canada to Central America, Caribbean

Hummingbird moth

This moth feeds on nectar, using its long feeding tube, or proboscis, to reach deep inside flowers. It hovers while it feeds, making a noise rather like the sound of a hummingbird's fast-beating wings. It may often be seen during the day but also flies at dusk and dawn.

Hummingbird moth

Family	Sphingidae
Latin name	*Macroglossum stellatarum*
Wingspan	2 in (5 cm)
Distribution	Europe, Asia

Noctuid moths and relatives

T he noctuid, or owlet, moth family is the largest of all the butterflies and moths, with more than 35,000 species all over the world. It also includes one of the biggest of all moths—the Agrippa moth. Most of these moths fly at night and are preyed on by bats, but many have special sense organs that pick up the bats' echolocation squeaks before they get too near. The caterpillars of many noctuids, and other similar moths, including clearwings and codling moths, cause damage to food crops.

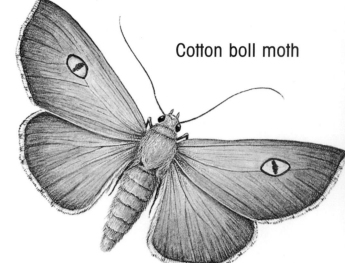
Cotton boll moth

Cotton boll moths

Most moths in this family fly at night and are dull in color. The cotton boll caterpillar feeds on cotton seedpods and can damage the plants.

Family	Noctuidae
Wingspan	Up to 2 in (5 cm)
Number of species	Over 35,000
Distribution	Worldwide

Agrippa moth

Also known as the birdwing moth and the white witch, this insect has one of the largest wingspans of any butterfly or moth, and dwarfs most other lepidopterans. It generally lives in forests where its mottled coloration helps it hide on lichen-covered tree trunks.

Family	Noctuidae
Latin name	*Thysania agrippina*
Wingspan	Up to 12$^1/_2$ in (32 cm)
Distribution	Mexico, Central and South America

Agrippa moth

Doll's clearwing moth

Family	Sesiidae
Latin name	*Paranthrene dollii*
Wingspan	Up to 1¹/₂ in (4 cm)
Distribution	Eastern U.S.A.

The wings of these moths have large patches without scales and therefore are at least partly transparent. The moths are generally active during the day and look similar to wasps as they fly from flower to flower. The female lays her eggs on trees. The larvae feed on bark and then burrow into the wood, which can damage the tree. In northern areas the caterpillars may live and feed for two years before pupating.

Doll's clearwing moth

Codling moth

The caterpillars of this moth are a pest of apple crops. The moth probably originated in Europe, but has now spread to apple-growing regions everywhere. The adults live in orchards and lay their eggs on leaves. When the larvae hatch they tunnel their way into young apples, where they feed on the seeds. They leave holes and brown trails inside the apple.

Codling moth

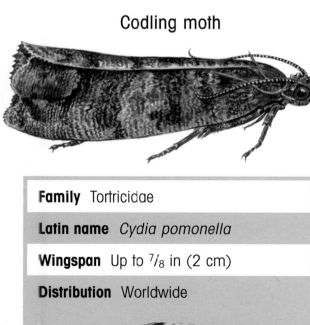

Family	Tortricidae
Latin name	*Cydia pomonella*
Wingspan	Up to ⁷/₈ in (2 cm)
Distribution	Worldwide

Family	Saturniidae
Latin name	*Actias luna*
Wingspan	Up to 4¹/₂ in (11.5 cm)
Distribution	Eastern North America, from southeast Canada to northern Mexico

Luna moth

This beautiful pale green moth has long tails that trail from its back wings. It lives in forests, and the caterpillars feed on the leaves of trees such as hickory, walnut, and birch. The caterpillars, which are green with yellow stripes, pupate in cocoons on the ground.

Luna moth

Burnet moths

Also known as smoky moths, the moths in this family are generally brightly colored and active during the day. They are slow fliers. The colorful markings of caterpillars and adults are a warning to birds and other predators that they taste nasty.

Burnet moth

Family	Zygaenidae
Wingspan	Up to 1¹/₈ in (2.8 cm)
Number of species	1,000
Distribution	Worldwide, more common in tropical areas

Monarch migration

One of the longest of all insect migrations is made by the monarch butterfly. These butterflies live in North America, but those in the north of their range cannot survive the cold winter. In the fall they start to build up fat to provide fuel for the journey ahead. In September, huge numbers fly south until they reach southern California or Mexico, where they cluster in vast numbers in trees through the winter. They return northward in spring, and lay their eggs on the first milkweed plants they find, then they die. Their offspring continue the journey north.

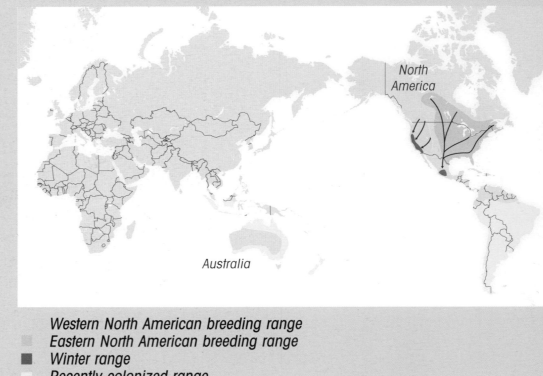

North America

Australia

Western North American breeding range
Eastern North American breeding range
Winter range
Recently colonized range
→ Fall migration route

Traveling insects

As most insects are such small, delicate creatures, it's hard to imagine them traveling very far. Many spend their whole lives on one plant. But a few, such as locusts and some kinds of dragonflies, beetles, and butterflies, do fly long distances—sometimes hundreds of miles—to escape cold weather, find good supplies of food, or colonize new areas.

Insect journeys

Some, such as painted lady butterflies, make yearly journeys called migrations. These journeys follow the same routes and are made at the same time every year. Dragonflies, hover flies, and locusts are among the insects that make less regular journeys to find food or living space. But migrations are not always by air. Army ants walk for long distances in columns of thousands. Caterpillars of the owlet moth family (Noctuidae) are often known as army worms because of their mass marches to find new feeding places.

Above The painted lady is one of the most widespread of all butterflies. Those living in areas with cold winters migrate to warmer zones in winter.

Locust swarms

From time to time, if their numbers increase significantly or if food becomes scarce, young locusts grow longer wings and develop brighter colors than the non-migrating locusts. Huge swarms of these locusts fly hundreds of miles across North Africa and the Middle East, destroying crops as they go. Swarms may contain millions of locusts—the biggest swarm ever may have numbered 10 billion!

Above A swarm of locusts flies away after destroying a crop field. A large swarm may spread over hundreds of square miles.

Swallowtail butterflies

Fluminense swallowtail

S ome of the largest and most beautiful of all butterflies belong to the Papilionidae family. It includes about 600 species found all over the world, except in Antarctica. Many are well known and easily recognized. All swallowtail caterpillars have a small forked structure behind the head. If disturbed the caterpillar lifts this structure, which smells terrible, to startle and put off the attacker.

Thoas swallowtail

The tail-like extensions on the wings of swallowtail butterflies may help to distract enemies from the vulnerable head area. Adults feed on nectar, while their caterpillars feed on citrus plants, as well as trees such as prickly ash. The caterpillars look rather like bird droppings as they lie on leaves—this helps them to avoid predators.

Family Papilionidae

Latin name *Papilio thoas*

Wingspan Up to 5 in (12.7 cm)

Distribution Southern North America, Central and South America to Brazil

Fluminense swallowtail

This beautiful butterfly is one of Brazil's most endangered insects. Loss of its swampy, bushy habitat, as a result of drainage for building and to provide banana plantations, has caused the species to die out in many areas. Conservationists hope to be able to catch some of these butterflies and establish new colonies in safer places.

Family Papilionidae

Latin name *Parides ascanius*

Wingspan Up to 4 in (10 cm)

Distribution Brazil

Thoas swallowtail

Cairns birdwing

The largest butterfly in Australia, these insects generally live in rainforests. The female is bigger than the male, but the male is more colorful. Adults feed on nectar, while the preferred food plant of the caterpillars is a vine called Dutchman's pipe. Birdwings are among the biggest butterflies in the world and are highly prized by collectors; many are now rare.

Cairns birdwing

Family	Papilionidae
Latin name	*Ornithoptera euphorion*
Wingspan	Up to 7 in (18 cm)
Distribution	Queensland, Australia

Queen Alexandra's birdwing

This huge butterfly lives in the dense rainforest of New Guinea. It was discovered in 1907 and named in honor of the British Queen Alexandra. As with other birdwings, the female is larger than the male, but is less colorful. She lays her eggs on plants called pipe vines and the caterpillars feed on the leaves of these plants. These butterflies are now rare, mostly because of the destruction of their rainforest home, but many are also trapped for sale to collectors. A female lays only 27 eggs in her life so these butterflies have a lower reproduction rate than many.

Queen Alexandra's birdwing

Family	Papilionidae
Latin name	*Ornithoptera alexandrae*
Wingspan	Up to 12 in (30 cm)
Distribution	Papua New Guinea

Apollo

Family	Papilionidae
Latin name	*Parnassius apollo*
Wingspan	Up to 3$\frac{1}{16}$ in (8 cm)
Distribution	Europe, central Asia

These rare butterflies are usually white with black and red markings. The caterpillars are black with orange-red spots. These butterflies usually live in high mountain pastures, where adults feed on the nectar of flowers such as stonecrop. The eggs are laid in early autumn and hatch the following spring. The caterpillars feed on stonecrop plants and pupate on the ground.

Apollo

Nymphalid butterflies and relatives

Morpho
butterfly

There are about 5,000 species of nymphalid butterflies living all over the world. They are most common in tropical areas. Nymphalids vary greatly in size and color, but in most the front legs are small and cannot be used for walking. Tipped with tiny tufts of hair, these legs look like tiny brushes—another name for these butterflies is brush-footed butterflies.

Monarch

Strong fliers, many of these butterflies make long migrations between summer breeding areas and warmer areas where they spend winter (see p. 124). Adults feed on the nectar of milkweed plants and caterpillars eat the leaves, which contain poisons that do not affect the monarch. These poisons make the caterpillar and butterfly taste nasty, and its bright colors are a warning to potential predators to find a meal elsewhere.

Family	Nymphalidae
Latin name	*Danaus plexippus*
Wingspan	Up to 5 in (12.5 cm)
Distribution	North, Central, and South America, Australasia, Europe

Monarch

Morpho butterflies

The morphos are some of the most brilliantly colored of all butterflies. Many are a brilliant, iridescent blue or green—the iridescence is caused by the arrangement of the rows of scales on the wings, which reflect the light. Females are usually plainer and duller than males. The males' bright coloration helps them attract mates, but also makes them obvious to predators. Fortunately, morphos are quick, agile fliers and are difficult to catch.

Family	Nymphalidae
Genus	*Morpho*
Wingspan	Up to 8 in (20 cm)
Distribution	Central and South America

Great
spangled
fritillary

Family	Nymphalidae
Wingspan	Up to 4 in (10 cm)
Latin name	*Speyeria cybele*
Distribution	Southwest Canada, northern U.S.A.

Great spangled fritillary

A large, boldly patterned butterfly, this fritillary varies in color over its range. Females in the western United States are much paler than those farther east. Adults feed on nectar from plants such as thistles and milkweeds. Females usually lay their eggs near violet plants. The caterpillars hibernate through the winter and then start to feed on violet leaves in spring. They feed only at night and remain hidden during the day.

Marbled white

This is a common butterfly on rough grassland and meadows. It is one of a group of butterflies known as the "browns." Adults feed on the nectar of plants such as thistles. They lay their eggs among grasses and the caterpillars hibernate through the winter. When spring arrives, they feed on the fresh, new grasses.

Family	Nymphalidae
Wingspan	Up to 3 in (7.6 cm
Latin name	*Vanessa atalanta*
Distribution	North and Central America, Europe, North Africa, Asia, New Zealand

Red admiral

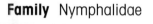

Family	Nymphalidae
Latin name	*Melanargia galathea*
Wingspan	Up to 2 in (5 cm)
Distribution	Europe, North Africa, Middle East

Marbled white

Red admiral

In northern areas, these fast-flying butterflies migrate south in winter to escape the cold. Adult red admirals feed on tree sap, juices from ripe fruit, and nectar. The caterpillars feed on nettle leaves and make themselves a shelter of leaves held together with silk.

Whites, metalmarks, and relatives

The whites (Pieridae) are a large family of butterflies. The family includes more than 1,000 species that live mostly in Africa and Asia. The Lycaenidae, or gossamer-winged butterfly family, is even larger. This is the second biggest butterfly family with 6,000 species. The metalmarks, with around 1,000 species, are closely related to the Lycaenidae. Skippers, with about 3,500 species, are thought to have features of both moths and butterflies.

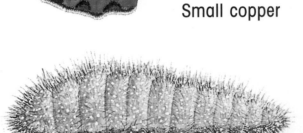

Small copper

Small copper caterpillar

Cabbage white

Cabbage white male

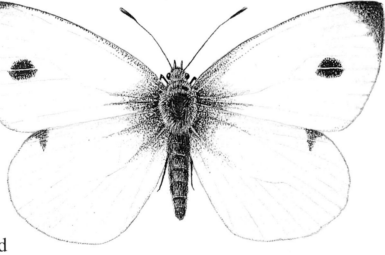

This is a very common butterfly, which has spread from Europe and Asia to North America, Australia, and New Zealand. Its wings are mostly white, and females have two dark spots on each, and males only one. Adults feed on nectar from plants, including dandelions and clover. The caterpillars eat plants of the cabbage family and are pests of cabbage, kale, and broccoli crops.

Family	Pieridae
Latin name	*Pieris rapae*
Wingspan	Up to 2¼ in (5.5 cm)
Distribution	North America, Europe, North Africa, Asia, Australasia

Cabbage white caterpillar

Family	Lycaenidae
Latin name	*Lycaena phlaeas*
Wingspan	Up to 1¼ in (3 cm)
Distribution	North America, Europe, North Africa, Asia

Small copper

The fiery colored copper often looks iridescent as it flutters around flowers feeding on nectar. In contrast, the fat and sluglike caterpillar is usually dull in color. Caterpillars eat the leaves of plants such as dock and sorrel.

Northern metalmark

Metalmark butterflies, many of which have metallic markings on their wings, are most common in tropical regions, but there are a couple of rare species in North America. Adults have a habit of landing on the underside of leaves where they rest. They also lay their eggs on the underside of leaves of plants such as ragwort.

Metalmark

Family	Riodinidae
Latin name	*Calephelis borealis*
Wingspan	Up to $1\frac{1}{4}$ in (3 cm)
Distribution	Eastern U.S.A.

Silver-spotted skipper

Silver-spotted skipper caterpillar

Family	Hesperiidae
Latin name	*Epargyreus clarus*
Wingspan	Up to $2\frac{1}{2}$ in (6 cm)
Distribution	North America, from southeast Canada to northern Mexico

Silver-spotted skipper

Skippers get their name from their fast, skipping style of flight. They have hook-tipped antennae and a sturdy body, rather like that of a moth. Adults are often seen perching on the underside of leaves. They feed on nectar, usually from blue, red, or purple flowers. Their caterpillars eat the leaves of plants, such as locust trees and wisteria. They feed only at night and stay hidden during the day.

Family	Pieridae
Latin name	*Colias eurydice*
Wingspan	Up to $2\frac{5}{8}$ in (6.5 cm)
Distribution	California

California dogface

This elegantly patterned butterfly is the state insect of California and has appeared on a U.S. postage stamp. Its dark wing markings are said to look like the profile of a dog's face, hence the species' common name. The caterpillar is green with orange-edged white markings. Its main food plant is the false indigo. Adults feed mostly on nectar from thistles.

California dogface

Below With eight eyes arranged in two or three rows, jumping spiders have better eyesight than most spiders. The large front eyes are particularly sensitive.

Spiders, scorpions, and relatives

Spiders and their relatives, such as scorpions and mites, are arachnids, not insects. They are an ancient group of animals, dating back some 400 million years. Arachnids have four pairs of legs and do not have wings or antennae. Although mites are the most abundant arachnids, spiders have the most species of the group.

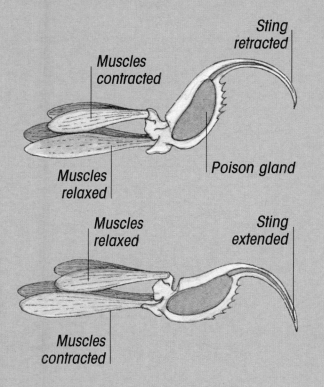

Sting retracted

Muscles contracted

Muscles relaxed

Poison gland

Muscles relaxed

Sting extended

Muscles contracted

Above The scorpion's sting is a hollow tube placed right at the end of the body it is connected to a poison supply. The squeezing action of muscles at the sting's base rocks it down into the tissues of the prey. Poison is forced down the tube by muscles around the gland.

Webs and stings

There are at least 40,000 known species of spider and many more are yet to be named. All spiders can make silk in the special glands at the end of the body, but not all species build webs; some spiders use silk to line their burrows and others make silken traps that they hold between their legs to snare prey. Young spiders use long strands of silk as parachutes to transport them to new territories—a technique called ballooning. Scorpions have a fearsome reputation and indeed some, such as the North African scorpion, have stings that can be fatal to humans. Other arachnids are harmless. Mites and ticks are tiny but occur in huge numbers. Some prey on insects while others live as parasites.

Spider life cycle

1 The female spider lays her eggs and protects them with a silken egg sac.
2 Some species leave their egg sacs to hatch on plants. Others place them on a web or carry them around with them. The young spiders, called spiderlings, hatch inside the egg sac. They grow and molt at least once before emerging from the sac.
3 When they emerge, the spiderlings look like tiny adults. They molt several times as they grow.
4 When they have grown sufficiently, the young spiders leave the home territory to find their own space in which to live, hunt, and reproduce.

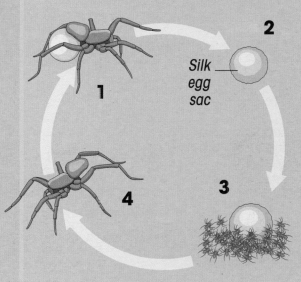

Silk egg sac

What are spiders and scorpions?

The arachnids are a group that includes spiders, scorpions, and mites. Like insects, they are adaptable and found all over the world in nearly every kind of habitat. There are at least 95,000, known species of arachnid, but there may be many more kinds of mite and tick yet to be discovered.

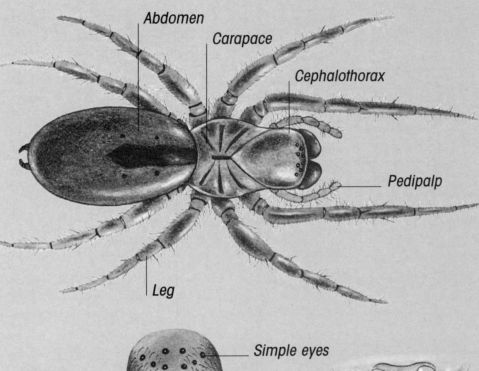

Spider anatomy

A typical spider's body is divided into two parts. The head and thorax are joined to make one structure called a cephalothorax. This is linked to the abdomen by a narrow waist. The cephalothorax is protected by a tough plate called the carapace. At the front of a spider's head are its jaws, called chelicerae. Behind these is the mouth. Nearly all spiders have venom glands, but only a few have a venomous bite that is dangerous to humans. Four pairs of legs are attached to the cephalothorax. The legs are divided into segments and are tipped with two or three claws. In front of the legs are the pedipalps, one on each side of the mouth. Males have larger pedipalps than females, which they use when mating. The abdomen contains most of the digestive and reproductive organs. The silk-making organs (spinnerets) are also in the abdomen.

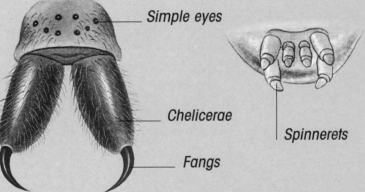

Above The detail of a spider's mouthparts shows the simple eyes, the chelicerae, or jaws, and the fangs. The spinnerets are the silk-producing organs.

Left A highly magnified image of a yellow mite. Although tiny, mites are extremely successful creatures. Some feed on plants, but others live as parasites on animals or plants.

| Animal Kingdom |
| Arthropoda |
| Arachnids |

Mites and ticks (Acari) 48,000 species

Spiders (Araneae) 40,000 species

Scorpions (Scorpiones) 1,300 species

Pseudoscorpions (Pseudoscorpionidae) 2,000 species

Sun spiders/wind scorpions (Solifugae) 900 species

Whip scorpions (Uropygi) 87 species

Harvestmen (Opilones) 4,500 species

Microwhip scorpions (Palpigradi) 60 species

Schizomids (Schizomida) 80 species

Ricinuleids (Ricinulei) 35 species

Below A scorpion's abdomen has two parts—the wider front section and a long "tail" with the sting at the end. When a scorpion attacks its prey, it swings the tail section forward over its body, bringing the sting into place.

Above The diagram above shows the main groups of arachnids. There are a number of different orders of mites and ticks but most do not have common names.

Mites and ticks

Mites and ticks are the smallest members of the arachnid group and are also the most numerous. There are about 48,000 species of mites and ticks living worldwide and there are probably many more to be discovered. They are extremely adaptable, living everywhere from the hottest to the coldest parts of the world: in deserts, on mountains, in polar regions, and in the deep sea. Many mites eat aphid eggs and prey on other small insects. Some also live as parasites on other animals, and a few eat plant foods. Ticks feed on the blood of animals.

House-dust mite

Velvet mites

These mites are named for the thick, soft hair that covers the rounded body and are some of the most colorful of all mites. They are common in soil and moss. Adult velvet mites feed mostly on insect eggs. They lay their eggs on the ground. When the larvae hatch, they live as parasites on insects and spiders, feeding on their body fluids.

Family	Trombidiidae
Length	$5/32$ in (4 mm)
Number of species	At least 3,000
Distribution	Worldwide

Velvet mite

House-dust mites

These tiny mites are very common in houses throughout the world, and feed on scales of skin found in house dust. Their droppings can contain materials that can cause allergic reactions, including asthma (difficulty in breathing), in susceptible people.

Family	Pyroglyphidae
Length	Up to $3/16$ in (5 mm)
Number of species	20
Distribution	Worldwide

Yellow mite

This fast-moving mite has piercing mouthparts that it uses to penetrate food sources such as plants and fungi. Some species of this family help plants, such as citrus trees, by feeding on the sooty mold fungus that can damage the trees.

Family	Tydeidae
Latin name	*Lorryia formosa*
Length	Up to $5/32$ in (4 mm)
Distribution	Worldwide

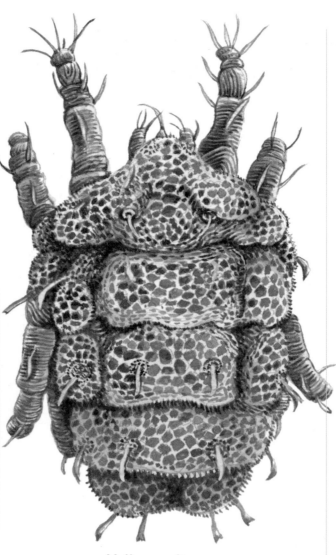

Yellow mite

Hard ticks

Hard ticks get their name from the hard shield that covers part of the front of the body. Like all ticks, they are parasites, feeding on the blood of animals. They cannot fly or jump and generally reach their hosts by clinging to plant stems and climbing onto any animal that brushes past. They stay on the host for several days while feeding, attached by their strong mouthparts. As they feed, some species pass on diseases such as Lyme disease. In fact, hard ticks probably spread more disease than any other group of invertebrates. The female lays eggs that hatch into six-legged larvae, which grow into nymphs with eight legs.

Hard tick

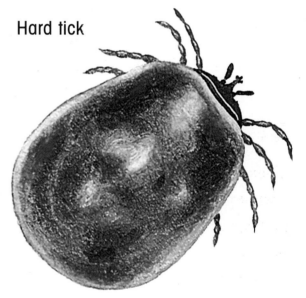

Family	Ixodidae
Length	Up to $1/8$ in (3 mm)
Number of species	650
Distribution	Worldwide

Soft ticks

Soft ticks do not have a hard body shield like that of hard ticks (right). They generally feed on the blood of birds, such as chickens and other poultry, and mammals, but do not usually bite humans. They like to live in the host's nest, moving onto the host to feed.

Family	Argasidae
Length	Up to $3/16$ in (5 mm)
Number of species	170
Distribution	Worldwide

Soft tick

Scorpions

This group includes the true scorpions, wind scorpions, and whip scorpions. There are about 1,300 species of true scorpion, most of which live in the warmer areas of the world. They use the venomous sting at the end of their body to kill prey and to defend themselves. A few kinds of scorpion have venom so powerful that it can kill a human, but the sting of most of these creatures is no worse than that of a bee or wasp. There are a number of smaller groups of scorpion relatives too, such as pseudoscorpions and harvestmen.

Family	Eremobatidae
Length	Up to 1³/₄ in (4.5 cm)
Number of species	187
Distribution	North and Central America

Wind scorpion

Buthid scorpions

These large scorpions hide under stones during the day and come out at night to seize insects and spiders in their powerful pincers. When the scorpion attacks its prey, it swings its sting forward over its body, bringing the sting into position to plunge into its victim. Scorpions have eyes but cannot see well. They find their prey mostly by touch, sensing movement via fine hairs attached to nerves on the body, legs, and claws. The female carries her newly hatched young around on her back for a few weeks until they are able to fend for themselves.

Family	Buthidae
Length	2–2³/₄ in (5–7 cm)
Number of species	528
Distribution	Tropical and warm temperate areas worldwide

Buthid scorpion

Wind scorpions

Wind scorpions, also known as sun spiders, are common in desert areas. These fast running hunters come out at night to prey on insects and even small lizards. They use their large pincers to catch prey. These can be as much as a third of the creature's total length and are some of the largest jaws relative to body size in the animal world.

Whip scorpions

Whip scorpions have a long, thin tail but no sting. They use the first pair of legs as feelers. The whip scorpion's other common name is vinegaroon because it sprays an acidic, vinegary liquid from glands near the base of its tail when frightened or disturbed. It hunts small creatures such as insects and millipedes at night.

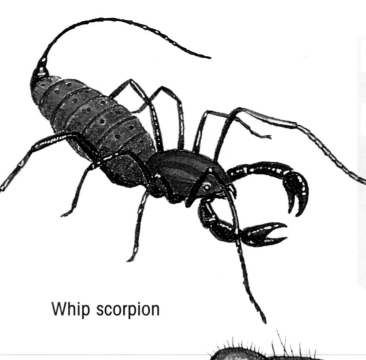

Whip scorpion

Family	Thelyphonidae
Length	Up to 1¼ in (3 cm)
Number of species	87
Distribution	Central and South America, Asia, Pacific Islands

Pseudoscorpion

Pseudoscorpion

These tiny soil-dwelling relatives of the scorpion have venom glands in their pincers, which they use when attacking prey. Pseudoscorpions also have silk glands, which enables them to spin cocoons in which to spend the winter. Some species perform courtship dances. The female then lays up to 40 eggs in a silk egg sac that she carries on her abdomen.

Family	Chernetidae
Length	¼ in (6 mm)
Number of species	650
Distribution	Worldwide

Harvestmen

Sometimes also known as daddy-long-legs, these arachnids have a rounded body without the narrow waist typical of spiders. All the legs are very long and thin but the second pair is the longest. Usually active at night, the harvestman hunts insects. If in danger, these insects may spray a foul-smelling liquid over the attacker. The female lays her eggs in the ground, where they stay through the winter until they hatch in the spring.

Family	Phalangiidae
Body length	½ in (1.3 cm)
Number of species	380
Distribution	Worldwide

Harvestman

Tarantulas and relatives

Spiders are extremely successful and adaptable creatures. They live all over the world in all kinds of habitats, except in Antarctica. The spiders on this page include some of the largest of the group.

Family	Theraphosidae
Latin name	*Brachypelma smithi*
Length	4 in (10 cm)
Distribution	Mexico

Red-kneed tarantula

Goliath bird-eating spider

The world's largest spider, this arachnid lives in tropical rainforest where it shelters in burrows in the ground. Despite its fearsome appearance, it isn't dangerous to humans. Its bite is not serious to us, and greater discomfort is caused by the irritation from the tiny hairs it can throw off its body when threatened. Unusually for spiders, when annoyed, the goliath can also make a hissing sound by rubbing its legs together. It does sometimes eat young birds, but more often it will feed on insects, mice, snakes, frogs, and lizards.

Family	Theraphosidae
Latin name	*Theraphosa blondi*
Legspan	Up to 12 in (30 cm)
Distribution	Northern South America

Goliath bird-eating spider

Red-kneed tarantula

Tarantulas are some of the largest of all spiders, with legs spanning more than 8 in (20 cm). Most hide during the day and come out at night to hunt insects and small creatures, which they kill with a venomous bite. Harmless to humans, they are popular pets.

Desert blond tarantula

This spider is named for the pale hairs on its back. It lives in deserts and hunts insects, lizards, and other small creatures, which it kills with its venomous bite. These spiders generally shelter in burrows, but when the male matures, at about three years of age, he sets out to find a female mate. Many males are caught by predatory wasps called tarantula hawks on their travels. The wasps paralyze the spiders and keep them next to their eggs as a food store for the larvae. Females lay their eggs on the ground in a sheltered hole or crevice.

Family	Theraphosidae
Latin name	*Aphonopelma chalcodes*
Length	Up to $2^3/_4$ in (7 cm)
Distribution	Southwest U.S.A., Mexico

Desert blond
tarantula

Funnel-web spiders

Spiders of this family make a funnel-shaped web that leads into an underground burrow. If a creature walks across the web, the spider senses the vibrations and rushes out for the kill. Funnel-webs prey on frogs and lizards, as well as insects. They have an extremely poisonous bite—the Sydney funnel-web is probably one of the most dangerous of all, with a bite that can kill humans. These spiders are not to be confused with the Agelenidae family of spiders found in North America, also known as funnel web weavers.

Funnel-web spider

Family	Dipluridae
Length	Up to $5/_8$ in (1.5 cm)
Number of species	175
Distribution	Subtropical and tropical regions worldwide

Trapdoor spiders

Trapdoor spiders have a special hunting technique: the spider digs a burrow with a hinged lid. It coats the inside of the burrow with a lining of earth, saliva, and silk. It then waits inside until it senses the movements of prey overhead through receptors in its legs. It then jumps out, grabs the prey, and takes it back to its burrow to eat.

Trapdoor spider

Family	Ctenizidae
Number of species	400
Body length	Up to $1^1/_4$ in (3 cm)
Distribution	Southwest U.S.A., southern Europe, Africa, Asia, Australia

Spitting spiders and relatives

Boreal comb-footed spider

Spiders put their silk-making abilities to a variety of uses. Many build a range of different types of web to catch prey, but others use silk to line their living quarters, wrap prey to keep it from escaping, and to protect their young or eggs.

Spitting spiders

These spiders get their name from their habit of spitting a sticky liquid to trap prey. They do not make webs and generally live on the ground and under stones, watching for insect prey. Once the prey is caught, the spider's bite turns the contents of its body to liquid that the spider can suck up at its leisure. The female carries her eggs until they hatch.

Family	Scytodidae
Body length	Up to $11/32$ in (9 mm)
Number of species	193
Distribution	Worldwide, except far north

Spitting spider

Comb-footed spiders

The spiders in this large family are also known as cobweb weavers. They spin large, irregular-shaped webs (often in the ceiling corners or around the windows of houses) and lie in wait for prey. If something gets caught, the spider adds more sticky threads, which it throws over the victim with the help of the small bristly combs on the end of the fourth pair of legs. The spider then kills the prey with its poisonous bite and takes it off to eat later.

Family	Theridiidae
Length	Up to $5/8$ in (1.5 cm)
Number of species	2,288
Distribution	Worldwide, excluding Arctic and Greenland

142

Wolf spiders

Fast-moving hunters like their namesakes, wolf spiders creep up on insect prey and seize it after a final speedy dash. Wolf spiders have good eyesight with their three rows of eight eyes, and this helps them find prey. They usually hunt at night and most do not make webs. A few dig burrows, lined with silk, where they shelter. A wolf spider's legs are covered with hair and tipped with three tiny claws.

Family Lycosidae

Length Up to 1 1/2 in (4 cm)

Number of species 2,336

Distribution Worldwide, excluding Arctic and Greenland

Wolf spider

Nursery web spiders

Nursery web spiders do not build webs to catch prey, but to protect their young. The female carries her egg sac with her until the eggs are almost ready to hatch. Then she spins a web over the eggs to protect them while they hatch. She stands guard nearby. These spiders live near water and sometimes hunt on the water surface as well as on plants.

Nursery web spider

Family Pisauridae

Length Up to 1 1/8 in (2.5 cm)

Number of species 336

Distribution Worldwide, excluding Arctic and Arabian Peninsula

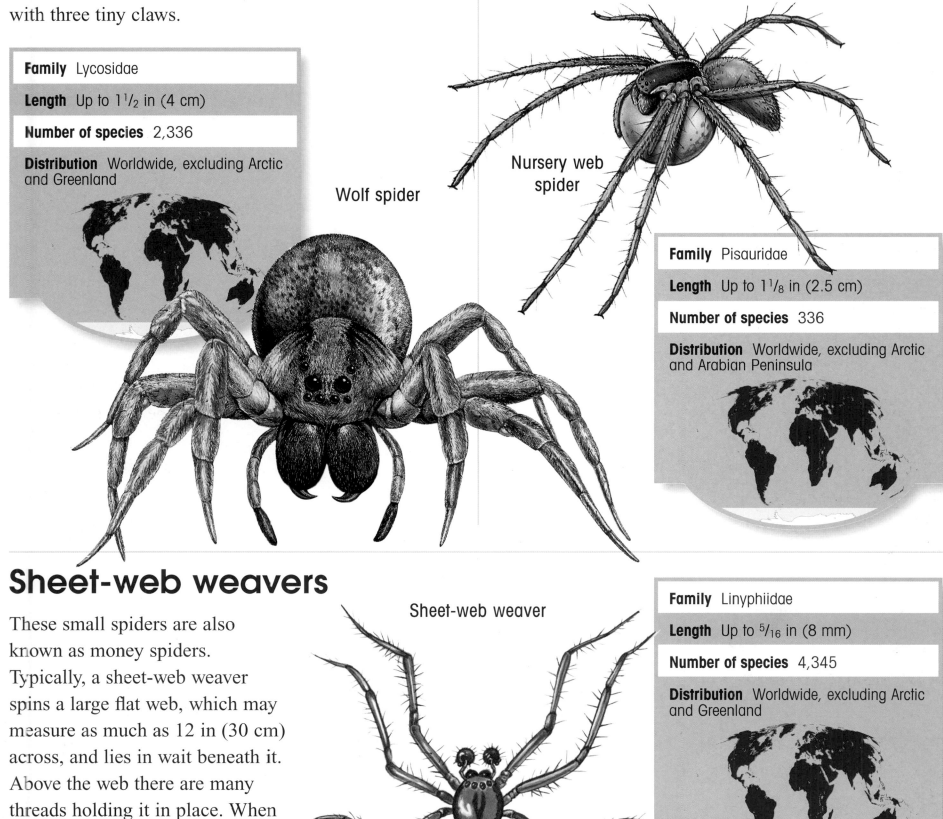

Sheet-web weavers

These small spiders are also known as money spiders. Typically, a sheet-web weaver spins a large flat web, which may measure as much as 12 in (30 cm) across, and lies in wait beneath it. Above the web there are many threads holding it in place. When a flying insect hits one of these threads, it falls down onto the sheet web, where it's grabbed from below by the spider.

Sheet-web weaver

Family Linyphiidae

Length Up to 5/16 in (8 mm)

Number of species 4,345

Distribution Worldwide, excluding Arctic and Greenland

Orb web spiders and relatives

The orb web spiders of the family Araneidae are some of the best-known of all spiders. Most make webs, but some such as the bolas spider have developed other ways of hunting. Funnel weavers and orchard spiders also make webs, and the water spider uses silk to make a diving bell.

Family	Argyronetidae
Latin name	*Argyroneta aquatica*
Length	Up to $^1/_2$ in (1.3 cm)
Distribution	Northern Europe

Funnel weavers

These spiders are a different family from the dangerous spiders known as funnel-web weavers (Dipluridae) (see p. 141). These spiders have long legs covered with strong bristles. They build large webs, sometimes slightly funnel-shaped, in any quiet corner of a house, garage, or shed. They then stay beneath the web waiting for prey to get tangled up in its sticky strands, which they then remove and eat the prey. A courting male may tap on a female's web before attempting to mate.

Family	Agelenidae
Length	Up to $^3/_4$ in (2 cm)
Number of species	511
Distribution	Worldwide

Funnel weaver

Water spider

This is the only spider that spends its whole life in water. It makes a special underwater shelter in which it can breathe air. Having spun a bell-shaped home of silk attached to water plants, the spider fills it with bubbles of air collected at the water surface. It then sits inside its bell, waiting for prey to come near. It pounces on the prey and takes it back to the bell to eat. Mating and egg-laying take place inside the bell.

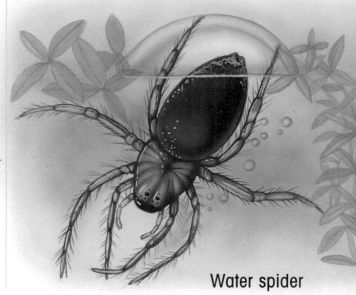

Water spider

Orchard spider

This colorful spider belongs to the large-jawed orb weaver family and has the large, strong jaws typical of its group. Not all spiders in this family make webs, but the orchard weaver makes a flattish web in bushes or small trees. It waits under the web or nearby for prey. Eggs are laid on leaves or twigs nearby.

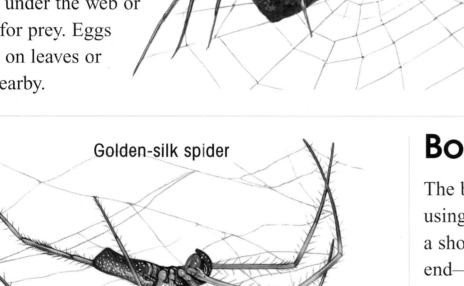

Orchard spider

Family	Tetragnathidae
Latin name	*Leucauge mabelae*
Length	Up to $5/16$ in (8 mm)
Distribution	North and Central America

Golden-silk spider

Golden-silk spider

These are some of the largest orb-weaving spiders. The female golden-silk spider is eight or nine times the length of the male and may weigh a hundred times as much. She is also much more colorful than the tiny dull brown male. The male's size is, in fact, an advantage when he approaches the female to try to mate with her. Like tiny insects that fly into her web, the male is too small to be worth attacking and is left alone. The female makes a large web up to 10 ft (1 m) across and waits beneath it for prey. The silk is deep yellow in color.

Family	Araneidae
Latin name	*Nephila clavipes*
Length	Up to $1^1/_2$ in (4 cm)
Distribution	Southeast U.S.A.

Bolas spider

The bolas spider has a particularly cunning way of using its silk to catch prey. It hunts at night and makes a short silken line with a sticky blob of silk at the end—rather like a fishing line with bait. If the spider hears a moth approaching, it twirls its line to attract the moth's attention. Amazingly, the lure contains a scent similar to that of a female moth so the moth investigates. If it gets too close, it sticks to the lure and is quickly reeled in to the spider's waiting jaws.

Family	Araneidae
Latin name	*Ordgarius magnificus*
Length	1 in (2.5 cm)
Distribution	Australia

Bolas spider

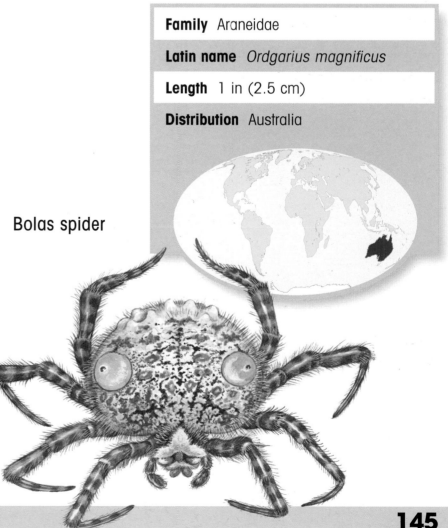

Jumping spiders and relatives

Some spiders, such as jumping spiders and lynx spiders, have good eyesight, but others rely more on their sense of touch to find prey and gain information about the world around them. Many spiders sense movement by tiny sensory hairs on the body and legs.

Jumping spider

Crab spiders

These spiders get their name from their habit of scuttling sideways like crabs. They rely heavily on camouflage when hunting, and do not make webs. Typically they sit on flowers and wait for pollinating insects to land on the petals. They then kill the prey with a poisonous bite. Many crab spiders are brightly colored to match the flowers they live on. Some males make use of their silk to tie females down before mating.

Family	Thomisidae
Length	Up to $^3/_8$ in (1 cm)
Number of species	2,085
Distribution	Worldwide

Yellow crab spider

Jumping spiders

Unlike many spiders, jumping spiders have good eyesight, which helps them find prey. Once it has spotted something, the spider leaps onto its victim. Before jumping, it attaches a silk thread to the ground as a safety line along which it can return to its hideout. Some can jump up to 50 times their own length. Jumping spiders do not make webs.

Family	Salticidae
Length	Up to $^5/_8$ in (1.5 cm)
Number of species	5,188
Distribution	Worldwide

Black widow

The female black widow has comblike bristles on her back legs, which she uses to throw strands of silk over prey that has become caught in her web. She has a venomous bite, which can be very painful to humans and needs immediate medical treatment. The male is much smaller than the female—only about $^5/_{32}$ in (4 mm) long. He does not bite and is generally eaten by the female after mating.

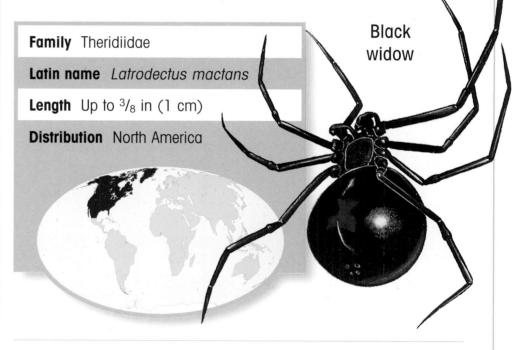

Black widow

Family	Theridiidae
Latin name	*Latrodectus mactans*
Length	Up to $^3/_8$ in (1 cm)
Distribution	North America

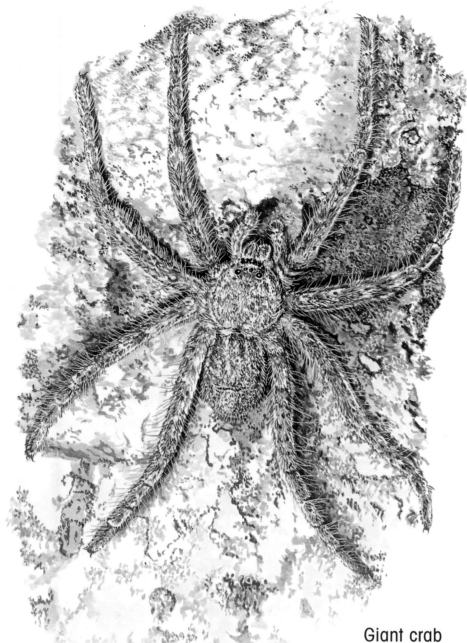

Giant crab spider

Giant crab spiders

Also known as huntsman spiders and wood spiders, many of the spiders in this family have mottled coloration that keeps them well hidden on lichen-covered tree bark. Tufts of tiny hairs on the legs break up any shadows, which might otherwise reveal their presence. If the spider suspects an enemy is near, it flattens itself against the bark, which makes it very difficult to see. They usually hunt at night, catching insects such as cockroaches.

Family	Sparassidae
Length	Up to $1^1/_8$ in (2.5 cm)
Number of species	1,038
Distribution	Worldwide, excluding Arctic

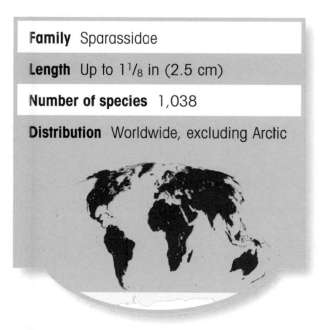

Lynx spiders

These long-legged spiders are fast-moving, active hunters. They do not build webs, but chase their prey over plants, jumping from leaf to leaf. They have good eyesight, which helps them spot their prey, and some are green to camouflage them among plants. The females spin silken egg sacs, which they attach to plants. They usually guard the eggs until they hatch.

Family	Oxyopidae
Length	Up to $^5/_8$ in (1.5 cm)
Number of species	426
Distribution	Worldwide, except far north of North America and Sahara Desert

Green lynx spider

Spider webs

Very few creatures build traps to catch their prey. Of those that do, among the best known are the orb-weaver spiders, which build the webs often seen in our houses and gardens. Spiders can make two types of silk from glands at the end of their body. One type hardens into a tough, non-sticky thread and is used to strengthen the web. The other is sticky and is used to trap prey.

Making a web

An orb-weaving spider starts by making a framework of non-sticky silk threads, using the breeze to help attach them to plants or other supports. It crawls along the threads, spinning more silk to add strength. It then adds "spokes" and spins a non-sticky spiral, starting from the center of the web. This spiral keeps the spokes separated so the spider can add the final part of the web. Starting at the outside, the spider then spins the sticky spiral that will trap prey, removing the non-sticky spiral as it goes. It leaves non-sticky spokes and a central hub in place so that it can walk around the web without becoming stuck. It waits nearby for prey to fly into its web. Once the prey is caught, the spider rushes over, bites it, and wraps it in strands of silk to prevent it from escaping.

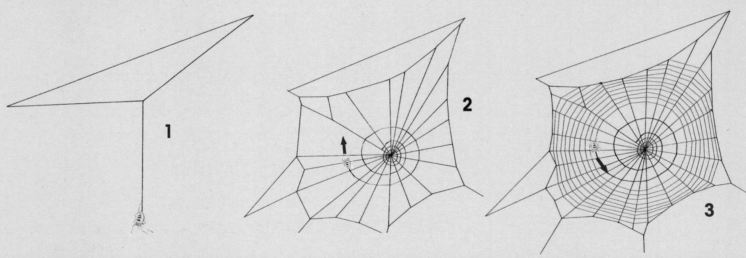

Left The stages in which a spider builds its web are:
1 Makes a framework of non-sticky threads.
2 Adds spokes and a non-sticky spiral.
3 Adds sticky spiral to trap prey.

The spitting spider

The spitting spider traps its prey by spitting out a sticky substance from glands near its mouth. It squirts this gum out in strands while moving toward its prey and turns its head from side to side so the strands criss-cross over the victim. Once the prey is pinned to the ground, the spider can feed at its leisure.

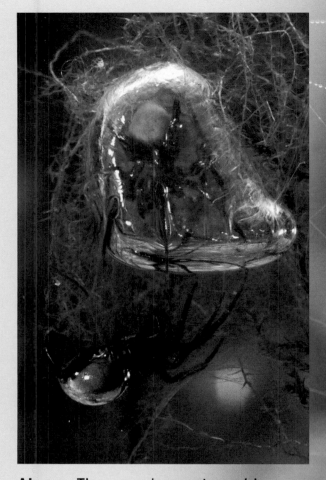

Above The amazing water spider makes an underwater diving bell of silk, which she fills with air bubbles. She catches prey in the water and takes it into her chamber to eat.

Left A black and yellow orb spider on her web. The decorative "braid" of silk below the spider may help to distract the spider's enemies, or may make the web more noticeable to larger creatures such as birds so that they avoid the web.

Above This garden orb weaver has trapped a dragonfly in her web and is busy wrapping the struggling prey in silken strands so it cannot escape.

Purse-web spiders and relatives

Spiders attack their prey with their strong jaws. On each jaw is a fang, linked to a poison gland. As the spider bites, venom flows through the fangs, paralyzes the victim, and also dissolves its body, creating a liquid meal that the spider can suck up with ease.

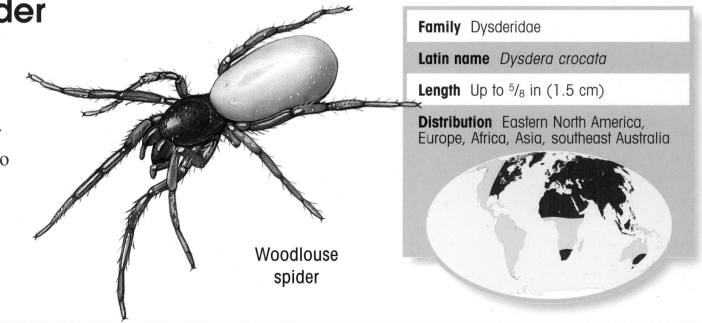

Purse-web spider

Purse-web spiders

Family Atypidae

Length Up to 1¼ in (3 cm)

Number of species 43

Distribution North America, Europe, North Africa, Asia

The purse-web spider builds a silken tube in a sloping burrow in the ground. The top of the tube extends above ground and is camouflaged with leaves. When an insect lands on the tube, the spider grabs it through the walls of the tube with its sharp fangs, and drags it inside. A courting male taps on a female's tube and may be allowed inside for mating. Eggs are laid inside the tube, where they remain through the winter and hatch in the spring.

Woodlouse spider

This spider has only six eyes—most spiders have eight—and extra-large fangs. It spends the day hiding under stones and come out at night to hunt woodlice. Woodlice have strong external skeletons, but this spider can pierce their armor with its sharp fangs.

Woodlouse spider

Family Dysderidae

Latin name *Dysdera crocata*

Length Up to ⅝ in (1.5 cm)

Distribution Eastern North America, Europe, Africa, Asia, southeast Australia

Net-casting spider

This spider, which has large eyes and excellent eyesight, takes its web to the prey. It makes a small but strong net of very sticky threads in a framework of dry silk. Once the trap is made, the spider hangs from a twig on silken lines, holding the net in its four front legs. When an insect comes near, the spider stretches the net wide so the prey flies into it and becomes entangled. The catch is then wrapped in the net and taken away to eat. There are similar spiders in South America and Asia.

Family	Deinopidae
Latin name	*Deinopis subrufa*
Length	1 1/8 in (2.5 cm)
Distribution	Southeast Australia

Head of net-casting spider

Net-casting spider

Ant-mimic spiders

These tiny spiders look like ants, move like ants, and often live near ant nests. This resemblance may lead predators to avoid them and helps the spiders get near to ants in order to catch them. They do not make webs but instead spin a silken tube inside a leaf or in a crack in a tree trunk or stone in which to rest safely. Females attach their egg sacs to stones.

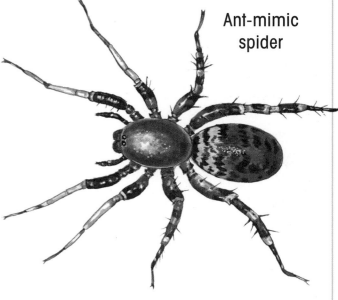

Ant-mimic spider

Family	Corinnidae
Genus	*Castianeira*
Length	Up to 3/8 in (1 cm)
Distribution	North America, Europe, Africa, Asia

Wandering spiders

These large, fast-moving spiders hunt prey on plants and on the ground. They do not make webs. Most live in tropical areas but some have spread into other regions in consignments of imported fruit, such as bananas. One Brazilian member of the family (Phoneutria) is very dangerous. It is one of the most poisonous spiders known and the most dangerous spider found in South America.

Family	Ctenidae
Length	Up to 1 1/2 in (4 cm)
Number of species	477
Distribution	North, South, and Central America, Africa, Asia, Australia

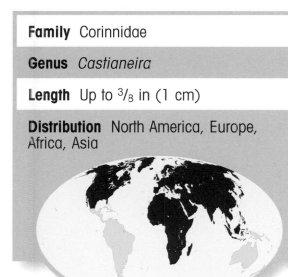

Brazilian wandering spider

Record breakers

Most insects and spiders are small, but there are some exceptions. A few can achieve astonishing feats of speed, jumping ability and strength. One of the most dangerous of all living creatures is the mosquito, which kills thousands of people every year because it carries diseases such as malaria.

Below The male Hercules beetle may be up to 6 $^3/_4$ in (17 cm) in length and has a huge horn extending over its head from the thorax. There is also a horn on the beetle's head. Males use their horns in battles with rivals.

Above A swarm of Asian tiger mosquitoes, which now live all over the world (except in Antarctica). This is an aggressive species; it flies and bites in the day as well as at night.

Biggest—and smallest

Of the insect giants, the longest are tropical stick insects or walking sticks. One Malaysian species grows to an incredible 18 inches (46 cm) in length, despite hatching from a tiny egg only $^5/_{32}$ inch (4 mm) long. Another giant is the titan beetle, the largest of all beetles at nearly 7 inches (18 cm) long. Its jaws are so strong that they can slice through human flesh! There are also a few beetles that, although not as long as this, are much heavier—for example, the African goliath beetle, which weighs up to $3^1/_2$ ounces (100 g). These beetle giants are also immensely strong and can lift about 850 times their own weight. The smallest insects are fairy flies, which measure less than $^1/_5$ mm.

Insect athletes

Many insect are great athletes. The tiny spittlebug can jump 100 times higher than its own length. Although only $^1/_{16}$ inch (2 mm) long, it can jump as high as 25 inches (64 cm)—that's like a person jumping over a skyscraper. The click beetle is less than ½ inch (1.3 cm) long but it springs into the air with greater force for its size than a space rocket taking off from earth. Dragonflies are some of the fastest flyers at 35 miles an hour (56 kph), and sun spiders can scuttle along on the ground at nearly 10 miles an hour (16 kph).

Right For their size, spittlebugs are the champion high-jumpers of the animal kingdom.

Danger!

There are dangerous and destructive insects and spiders, too. The desert locust probably causes more damage to crops than any other living creature. Huge swarms can destroy whole fields of grain. Humans can be killed by the sting of a honeybee, but the insect with the most powerful venom is the harvester ant. The most venomous spider is probably the Brazilian wandering spider. Just a tiny amount (0.006 mg) of its venom is enough to kill a mouse. Another very dangerous spider is the Sydney funnel-web spider, which has been known to cause deaths in humans.

Above The Brazilian wandering spider has probably caused more human deaths than any other species of spider.

Glossary

Abdomen
Part of an insect's body, located behind the head and thorax.

Antennae
A pair of slender, sensitive structures on an insect's head. Antennae help an insect smell, taste, and touch things around it.

Arachnid
An arthropod with eight legs. Spiders, scorpions, ticks, and mites are all arachnids.

Camouflage
The colors or patterns on an animal's body that help it blend in with its surroundings so it cannot easily be seen by enemies or prey.

Carrion
The bodies of dead animals.

Caterpillar
The larva of a moth or butterfly.

Cell
A six-sided compartment in the nest of a bee or wasp that is often used for storing food or eggs.

Cephalothorax
The part of a spider's body that comprises the head and thorax.

Chelicerae
Jaws at the front of the head of a spider or scorpion.

Cocoon
A silky case spun by an insect larva to protect itself while in the pupal stage (see Pupa).

Colony
A group of individuals of a single species living together in one place. Ants, termites, and some bee and wasp species live in colonies.

Compound eyes
Eyes that are made up of hundreds of different parts, each of which has a tiny lens on the surface.

Courtship
Animal behavior that leads to the choosing of a mate and mating.

Family
A group of related genera, which are themselves groups of related species. The scientific name of a family usually ends in –idae.

Fangs
Pointed mouthparts, sometimes used to inject venom into prey.

Fungi
Simple living things that are not green plants and not animals. Mushrooms are types of fungi.

Gall
A growth that forms on a plant, around the eggs of some kinds of wasps and other insects.

Gland
A part of the body that produces special substances, such as poisons.

Halteres
The hind wings of a fly, which are reduced to a pair of small, knobbed structures. Halteres help the fly to maintain balance during flight.

Host
An animal that has a parasite, such as a flea, living and feeding on or in it.

Invertebrate
An animal without a backbone. Insects, spiders, and scorpions, as well as creatures such as slugs, snails, crabs, and clams, are invertebrates.

Larva
A juvenile form of a creature, which hatches from an egg. A larva looks quite different from the adult animal. A caterpillar, for example, is the larva of a butterfly.

Mammal
A warm-blooded animal, usually four-legged and hairy, that gives birth to fully formed young. Female mammals feed their young on milk, a nutritious secretion produced by their mammary glands.

Mating
The coming together of male and female creatures to produce young.

Metamorphosis

A marked change in form from one stage in a life cycle to the next, such as from caterpillar to pupa, and pupa to butterfly.

Migration

The periodic passage of groups of animals from one region to another for feeding or breeding.

Molt

To shed an outer covering, such as a larval skin, that will be replaced by a new growth.

Nectar

A sugary liquid made by plants that attracts insects.

Nymph

The larval form of certain insects—for example, grasshoppers—which usually resemble the adult form but are somewhat smaller and lack fully developed wings.

Order

A group of related families.

Ovipositor

The egg-laying tube that is situated at the end of a female insect's abdomen.

Paralyze

To affect an animal's nervous system so that it cannot move, but is still alive.

Parasite

An organism that lives on or in, and does harm to, its host—an organism of another species.

Pedipalps

Projecting sense organs in arachnids. Some arachnids use pedipalps to grasp objects such as prey.

Pollen

Fine powder inside a flower that fertilizes other flowers of that species; usually colored yellow.

Predator

A creature that hunts and kills other creatures for food.

Prey

An animal that is hunted and eaten by other animals.

Pupa

The stage in the life cycle of some insect species during which they change from a larva into an adult.

Queen

An egg-laying female in a colony of ants, bees, wasps, or termites.

Rainforest

Forests near the equator that are hotter and wetter than other forests.

Silk

Protein threads made by spiders and some insects.

Species

A type of animal. Living things of the same species can mate and produce young that in turn are able to have young.

Spinnerets

The fine tubes at the end of a spider's abdomen. Silk for spinning a web comes out of the spider's body through the spinnerets.

Territory

An area that an animal defends against intruders.

Thorax

Part of an insect's body, between the head and abdomen. An insect's legs are attached to the thorax.

Venom

A liquid made by an insect or arachnid that is used to kill or paralyze prey.

Web

A network of silken threads woven by a spider and used to trap prey.

Wing cases

The hard coverings that are formed by a beetle's front wings and used to protect its back wings.

Workers

The insects in a social colony that build the nest, find food, and care for young.

Index

Index

Acknowledgments

Illustrators

Robin Boutell, Joanne Cowne, Sandra Doyle, Bridget James, Steve Kirk, Adrian Lascombe, Alan Male, Colin Newman, Steve Roberts, Bernard Robinson, Roger Stewart, Gill Tomblin, Colin Woolf

Marshall Editions would like to thank the following for their kind permission to reproduce their images:

b = bottom **c** = center **t** = top **l** = left **r** = right

All images inside this book (except 134b) are reproduced courtesy of FLPA (www.flpa.co.uk) and its associate agencies.

Pages: 1 Ingo Arndt/Minden Pictures; **2–3** Jurgen & Christine Sohns; **4–5** Wendy Dennis; **7** Konrad Wothe/Minden Pictures; **8–9** Derek Middleton; **9cr** Martin B Withers; **10tr** Mitsuhiko Imamori/Minden Picture; **11r** Derek Middleton; **12bl** Nigel Cattlin; **12tr** Siegfried Grassegger/Imagebroker; **13t** Andrè Skonieczny/Imagebroker; **13c** Parameswaran Pillai Karunakaran; **13br** Bob Gibbons; **14–15** Pete Oxford/Minden Pictures; **16–17** Cisca Castelijns/Foto Natura; **17tr** Rene Krekels/Foto Natura; **22** Michael Durham/Minden Pictures **23** Andrè Skonieczny/Imagebroker; **26** Michael Durham/Minden Pictures; **27t** Michael & Patricia Fogden/Minden Pictures; **40** Albert Visage; **40–41** Mitsuaki Iwago/Minden Pictures; **41cr** Fritz Polking; **46** Ingo Arndt/Minden Pictures; **47t** Ingo Arndt/Minden Pictures; **54t** Michael & Patricia Fogden/Minden Pictures; **55l** Ingo Arndt/Foto Natura/Minden Pictures; **55r** Pete Oxford/Minden Pictures; **60t** Martin B Withers; **60b** Sunset; **68–69t** Michael & Patricia Fogden/Minden Pictures; **69b** Michael Durham/Minden Pictures; **74–75** Konrad Wothe/Minden Pictures; **75cr** Nigel Cattlin; **81t** Mark Moffett/Minden Pictures; **86b** Albert Visage; **87b** T S Zylva; **87t** David Hosking; **94t** Nigel Cattlin; **94b** Konrad Wothe/Minden Pictures; **100bl** Phil McLean/Holt Studios; **100–101** Frans Lanting; **101r** Christian Ziegler/Minden Pictures; **102** Foto Natura Stock; **108–109bc** Larry West; **108tr** Michael & PatrickFogden/Minden Pictures; **109tr** Michael Gore; **116bc** Mitsuhiko ImamoriI/Minden Pictures; **117bl** Andrea Denotti/Foto Natura/Minden Pictures; **124** Frans Lanting; **125b** Mitsuhiko ImamoriI/Minden Pictures; **132** Marak Moffett/Minden Pictures; **134b** Agricultural Research Service © Eric Erbe/digital colorization by Chris Pooley: www.ars.usda.gov; **135** Frans Lanting; **149tl** Silvestris Fotoservice; **149bl** Neil Bowman; **149r** Bob Gibbons; **152c** Mark Moffett/Minden Pictures; **152–153b** Mitsuhiko Imamori/Minden Pictures